The Transferring of America's Youth

The Transferring of America's Youth

Edited by
Sheri Jenkins Keenan

LEXINGTON BOOKS
Lanham • Boulder • New York • London

Published by Lexington Books
An imprint of The Rowman & Littlefield Publishing Group, Inc.
4501 Forbes Boulevard, Suite 200, Lanham, Maryland 20706
www.rowman.com

6 Tinworth Street, London SE11 5AL, United Kingdom

British Library Cataloguing in Publication Information Available

Library of Congress Cataloging-in-Publication Data

Name: Keenan, Sheri Jenkins, 1970– editor.
Title: The Transferring of America's Youth / edited by Sheri Jenkins Keenan.
Description: Lanham : Lexington Books, 2021. | Includes bibliographical references and index. | Summary: "This volume provides a comprehensive historical review of the transferring of American's youth from the rehabilitative, individualized treatment of the juvenile justice system into the adult criminal justice system"—Provided by publisher.
Identifiers: LCCN 2021028370 (print) | LCCN 2021028371 (ebook) | ISBN 9781793623638 (cloth) | ISBN 9781793623645 (epub)
Subjects: LCSH: Juvenile justice, Administration—United States. | Juvenile delinquents—Legal status, laws, etc.—United States. | Juvenile courts—United States. | Juvenile delinquents—Rehabilitation—United States. | Criminal justice, Administration of—United States. | Criminal courts—United States. | Criminal procedure—United States.
Classification: LCC KF9812 .T76 2021 (print) | LCC KF9812 (ebook) | DDC 345.73/08—dc23
LC record available at https://lccn.loc.gov/2021028370
LC ebook record available at https://lccn.loc.gov/2021028371

Contents

Introduction

Sheri Jenkins Keenan

Fifty years ago, juvenile justice policy debates focused on issues concerning decriminalization of status offenses, due process for juveniles, deinstitutionalization, and diversion (Bernard, 1992; Howell, 1996; McCord, Widom & Crowell, 2001; Siegel & Welsh, 2009). Currently, juvenile justice policy debates are focused on the question of whether serious, violent, and chronic juvenile offenders should remain in the juvenile justice system or be transferred to the adult criminal justice system (Bernard, 1992; Howell, 1996).

Before the 1800s, the United States had no juvenile justice system (Elton & Roybal, 2003; Empey, 1978; Finestone, 1976; Houston & Barton, 2005; Howell, 1997; National Research Council Staff, 2000; Schwartz, 1989). Criminal cases involving juveniles were handled in adult criminal court (Finestone, 1976; Howell, 1997; Schwartz, 1989; Thornton & Voigt, 1992). Juveniles who were convicted of crimes were subject to the same sanctions as adults (Siegel & Welsh, 2009; Thornton & Voigt, 1992).

A separate juvenile justice system was established in the United States in 1899 with the formation of the nation's first juvenile court in Chicago, Illinois (Bernard, 1992; Fox, 1996; Houston & Barton, 2005; Howell, 1997; Ryerson, 1978; Siegel & Welch, 2009; Schwartz, 1989). The goal of the new juvenile court was to divert juvenile offenders from the harsh punishments of the adult criminal court, and encourage rehabilitation based on the individual needs of the juvenile. This new juvenile court differed from the adult criminal court in several ways. First, the new juvenile court focused on the juvenile as a person in need of assistance, not on the act that brought him or her before the court. In addition, the new juvenile court was set up as a civil or chancery court intended to serve the best interests of the juvenile offender as opposed to the adult criminal court, which focused on the punishment of offenders. Because the new juvenile court was set up as a civil court the proceedings were informal with discretion left to the juvenile court judge. Procedural safeguards available to adults were thought to be unnecessary (Gold, 2007). Furthermore, juvenile court proceedings were closed to the public, and juvenile records were to remain confidential. To further distinguish the differences between the new juvenile court and the adult criminal court, the very terminology used was changed. Juveniles did not commit crimes but acts of delinquency. They were not criminals, but delinquents. Juveniles were not arrested; they were taken into custody. They were not detained in jails, but detention centers and shelter care. The juvenile justice system does not have bail hearings, but detention hearings. Adjudicatory hearings take the place of trials. Juveniles are not found guilty; they are adjudicated delinquent. Juveniles do not plead guilty or not guilty, but rather true or not true. The sentencing phase of the adjudicatory hearing in juvenile court is called the disposition hearing. Juveniles are not punished, they are rehabilitated. They are not incarcerated in facilities and programs, but committed to, or placed in, facilities and programs. Finally, juveniles are not sent to prisons, but to training schools and reformatories. Parole is called aftercare (Sanborn & Salerno, 2005).

For the most part, the period between the establishment of the nation's first juvenile court in 1899 and the early 1960s was marked by little change in how juvenile delinquency was defined, or what activities constituted delinquent conduct. The juvenile justice system operated under the medical model (Taylor, Fritsch & Caeti, 2007), and the goal of a juvenile proceeding was to cure a wayward juvenile. However, as the decades progressed, juveniles became increasingly involved in more serious crimes.

In the 1960s, legal and public concern about juvenile delinquency took a sharp turn as delinquency rates rose to alarming levels. Not only were juveniles being arrested for the traditional minor property crimes, mischief, and status offenses, but also for murder, forcible rape, aggravated assault, and robbery (Cook & Laub, 1998; Sickmund et al., 1998). Alarming statistics helped foster the increasing fear of juveniles among adults. Some states responded with new policies whereby juveniles who posed a serious threat to the community would be treated as adults (McCord et al., 2001).

By the early 1970s, many states had adopted legislation that redefined the noncriminal behavior of juveniles. New statutes were written to clarify the distinctions between status offenses, dependency, and neglect. In 1976, the National Advisory Committee of Criminal Justice Standards and Goals recommended that status offenses be limited to only five specific categories: school truancy, repeated disregard for or misuse of lawful parental authority, repeated running away from home, repeated use of intoxicating beverages, and delinquent acts committed by a juvenile younger than ten years of age (McCord et al., 2001). Similarly, the International Association of Chiefs of

Police (IACP) suggested that the term "juvenile delinquent" be reserved for juveniles who commit criminal offenses and who are in need of supervision or treatment (Armstrong, 1977; Chesney-Lind, 1970; McCord et al., 2001). The IACP suggested that the term "unruly child" be applied to juveniles who commit status offenses, are ungovernable or habitually truant from school, and are in need of treatment for those problems (Armstrong, 1977; Chesney-Lind, 1970; McCord et al., 2001).

In the late 1980s and early 1990s, the dramatic rise in juvenile violence generated considerable fear and concern among lawmakers, educators, law enforcement, and the general public, and led to policy changes by federal, state, and local governments (Bennett, Dilulio & Walters, 1996; Blumstein, 1995; Blumstein & Cork, 1996; Blumstein & Rosenfeld, 1998; Fagan & Wilkinson, 1998; Griffin, Addie, Adams, & Firestine, 2011; Sickmund, Snyder & Poe-Yamagata, 1997; Zimring, 1998). For example, juvenile violent crime arrest rates increased by more than 60 percent from 1988 to 1994 (Snyder, 1998), and the murder arrest rate for juveniles rose by more than 100 percent over this same period (Cook & Laub, 1998; Zimring, 1998). In addition to the rise in violent juvenile crime rates, violent victimization of juveniles was also on the rise. It appeared that juveniles were not only becoming more involved in violent acts but were also suffering at the hands of their peers. Serious and violent juvenile delinquents started to be labeled "super-predators" (Dilulio, 1995, p. 23), because they were thought to be more dangerous than previous generations of juvenile offenders (Bennett et al., 1996; Dilulio, 1995).

As a result of growing public concern about juvenile violence, legislatures and juvenile courts responded with a number of get-tough policies and strategies (Taylor, Fritsch & Caeti, 2002). The rise in public concern that led to these get-tough policies was fueled by what Samuel Walker (1994), in his book, *Sense and Nonsense about Crime and Drugs A Policy Guide*, called celebrated cases. Walker (1994) proposed a model of justice that divides the criminal justice process into four layers; the layers of a wedding cake, based on the seriousness and notoriety of the crime.

The first layer of Walker's (1994) wedding cake model was made up of the celebrated cases involving the wealthy, the famous, and those cases that were widely reported in the media (Walker, 1994). Cases in the first layer of the wedding cake model usually received the entire muster of criminal justice procedures: competent defense attorneys, expert witnesses, jury trials, and elaborate appeals (Walker, 1994). The mainstream media focuses on level one cases, thus giving the general public the false impression that criminals are sober, intelligent people, and victims are members of the upper class (Walker, 1994). The result is that public opinion regarding crime and victimization is formed on the basis of what happened in an atypical case.

The second layer of Walker's (1994) wedding cake model is made up of serious felonies: rape, robbery, and burglary. These crimes are placed on the second level because they are crimes committed by experienced offenders and are routine in our everyday society. The police, prosecutors, and judges all agree that these are serious crimes worthy of the full attention of the criminal justice system. Offenders who commit second layer offenses receive a jury trial and, if convicted, receive prison sentences.

The third layer of Walker's (1994) wedding cake model consists of less serious felonies committed by juveniles, first-time offenders, or involves people who knew each other or were related. Criminal justice practitioners relegate these cases to the third level because they view them as less important and less deserving of attention. Third layer crimes are dealt with by dismissals, plea bargains, reduced charges, and probationary sentences.

The fourth and final layer of Walker's (1994) wedding cake model consists of millions of misdemeanors: disorderly conduct, shoplifting, public intoxication, and so on. The lower criminal courts handle these cases in assembly-line fashion. In this fourth level, few defendants exercise their constitutional rights because the delay would cost the defendant time and money. The typical penalty for level four crimes is a fine.

In the 1990s, the most popular approach in dealing with violent juvenile crime was for states to make it easier or to require the prosecution of juveniles as adults in criminal court (Griffin et al., 2011; Torbet et al., 1996). Although waiving juveniles to the adult criminal court actually has been in de facto existence since the early 1800s, it was reserved for small numbers of the most serious and violent juvenile offenders. Modern waiver laws sought to change and increase the use of this practice by reducing judicial discretion in juvenile court, enhancing prosecutorial power to file charges directly in adult court, and statutorily excluding certain offenses and offenders from the juvenile court jurisdiction. The underlying rationale was that greater use of juvenile waiver would boost accountability and punishment, and thus would reduce juvenile crime.

Juvenile crime rates have declined steadily since 1994; however, the high visibility of a select number of violent crimes by juveniles has caused public concern and legislative action (McCord et al., 2001; Synder, 2002). Some policymakers have claimed that the declines in juvenile crime rates are a result of the get-tough policies and sanctions. Despite the questionable impact of harsher laws and penalties on juvenile offending, providing more severe punishments for serious and violent juvenile offenders continues to receive political and public support, and waiver laws enacted during the 1990s remain in place.

All states and the District of Columbia now use at least one of the three mechanisms that allow juveniles to be waived to the adult criminal justice system (Torbet & Szymankski, 1998; NCJFCJ, 2006). The procedures for waiver vary across states, but usually a combination of factors are considered: the seriousness of the offense; the need to protect the community; whether the offense was committed in an aggressive, violent, premeditated, or willful manner; whether the offense was against a person or property; the merit of the complaint; whether the juvenile's associates will be tried in adult criminal court; the juvenile's sophistication, maturity, record, and previous history; and the reasonable likelihood of rehabilitation (Griffin, Torbet, & Szymanski, 1998; NCJFCJ, 2006; Torbet & Szymanski, 1998).

REFERENCES

Armstrong, G. (1977). Females under the law: Protected but unequal. *Crime and Delinquency, 23*, 109–120.

Bernard, T. J. (1992). *The cycle of juvenile justice.* New York: Oxford University.

Bennett, W. J., Dilulio, J. J., & Walters, J. P. (1996). *Body count: Moral poverty and how to win America's war against crime and drugs.* New York: Simon and Schuster.

Blumstein, A. (1995). Youth violence, guns and the illicit-drug industry. *The Journal of Criminal Law and Criminology, 86*(1), 10–36.

Blumstein, A., & Cork, D. (1996). Linking gun availability to youth gun violence. *Law and Contemporary Problems, 59*(1), 5–37.

Blumstein, A., & Rosenfeld, R. (1998). Explaining recent trends in U.S. homicide rates. *The Journal of Criminal Law and Criminology, 88*(4th), 1175–1216.

Chesney-Lind, M. (1970). Judicial paternalism and the female status offender. *Crime and Delinquency, 23,* 121–130.

Cook, P. J., & Laub, J. H. (1998). The unprecedented epidemic in youth violence. In M. Tonry & M. H. More (Eds.), *Crime and justice: A review of research* (pp. 27–64). Chicago, IL: University of Chicago.

Dilulio, J. J. (1995). The coming of the super-predators. *Weekly Standard, 1*, 23–28.

Elton, K., & Royball, M. M. (2003). Restoration, a component of justice. *Utah Law Review, 42*, 43–56.

Empey, L. T. (1978). *American delinquency: Its meaning and construction.* Homewood, IL: Dorsey.

Fagan, J., & Wilkinson, D. L. (1998). Guns, youth violence, and social identity. In M. Tonry & M. H. More (Eds.), *Youth violence: Crime and justice* (pp. 105–188). Chicago, IL: University of Chicago.

Finestone, H. (1976). *Victims of change: Juvenile delinquents in American society.* Westport, CT: Greenwood.

Fox, S. J. (1996, Winter). The early history of the court. *The Future of Children The Juvenile Court, 6*(3), 29–39.

Gold, S. D. (2007). *In re Gault: Do minors have the same rights as adults?* New York: Marshall Cavendish Benchmark.

Griffin, P., Addie, S., Adams, B., & Firestine, K. (2011). *Trying juveniles as adults: An analysis of state transfer laws and reporting* (Office of Juvenile Justice and Delinquency Prevention No. 232434). Washington, DC: U.S. Department of Justice.

Griffin, P., Torbet, P., & Szymanski, L. (1998). *Trying juveniles as adults in criminal court: An analysis of state transfer provisions* (Office of Juvenile Justice and Delinquency Prevention No. NCJ- 172836). Washington, DC: U. S. Department of Justice.

Houston, J., & Barton, S. M. (2005). *Juvenile justice theory, systems, and organization.* Upper Saddle River, NJ: Prentice Hall.

Howell, J. C. (1996). Juvenile transfers to the criminal justice system: State of the art. *Law and Policy, 18*, 17–60.

Howell, J. C. (1997). *Juvenile justice and youth violence.* Thousand Oaks, CA: Sage.

McCord, J., Widson, K. S., & Crowell, N. A. (2001). Juvenile Crime, Juvenile Justice: Panel on Juvenile Crime: Prevention, Treatment, and Control. Washington, DC: National Research Council. https://www.ojp.gov/ncjrs/virtual-library/abstracts/juvenile-crime-juvenile-justice-panel-juvenile-crime-prevention

National Research Council Staff. (2000). *Juvenile crime, juvenile justice.* Washington, DC: National Academies Press, 154–227.

National Research Council and Institute of Medicine. (2001). *Juvenile Crime, Juvenile Justice.* Washington, DC: The National Academies Press. https://doi.org/10.17226/9747.

NCJFCJ. (2006, January 1). Juvenile Justice Reform Initiatives in the states 1994–1996. In *Juvenile transfer to criminal court.* Washington, DC: U. S. Department of Justice.

Ryerson, E. (1978). *The best-laid plans America's juvenile court experiment.* New York: Hill and Wang.

Sanborn, J. B., & Salerno, A. W. (2005). *The juvenile justice system law and process.* Los Angeles, CA: Roxbury.

Schwartz, I. M. (1989). *Justice for juveniles rethinking the best interests of the child.* Lexington, MA: Lexington University.

Sickmund, M., Snyder, H., & Poe-Yamagata, E. (1997). *Juvenile offenders and victims: 1997 update on violence* (Office of Juvenile Justice and Delinquency Prevention). Washington, DC: U. S. Department of Justice.

Sickmund, M., Stahl, A. L., Finnegan, T. A., Snyder, H. N., Poole, R. S., & Butts, J. A. (1998). *Juvenile court statistics, 1995* (Office of Juvenile Justice and Delinquency Prevention). Washington, DC: U. S. Department of Justice.

Siegel, L. J., & Welsh, B. C. (2009). *Juvenile delinquency theory practice and law.* Belmont, CA: Wadsworth.

Snyder, H. N. (1998). *Juvenile arrest 1997* (Office of Juvenile Justice and Delinquency Prevention No. NCJ 173938). Washington, DC: U. S. Department of Justice.

Snyder, H. N. (2002). *Juvenile arrests 2000* (Office of Juvenile Justice and Delinquency Prevention No. NCJ- 191729). Washington, DC: U. S. Department of Justice.

Taylor, R. W., Fritsch, E. J., & Caeti, T. J. (2002). *Juvenile justice: Policies programs and practices.* Woodland Hills, CA: Glencoe/McGraw-Hill.

Taylor, R. W., Fritsch, E. J., & Caeti, T. J. (2007). *Juvenile justice policies programs, and practices* (2nd ed.). New York: McGraw-Hill.

Thornton, W. E., & Voigt, L. (1992). *Delinquency and justice.* New York: McGraw-Hill.

Torbet, P., Gable, R., Hurst, H. I., Montgomery, I., Szymanski, L., & Thomas, D. (1996). *State Responses to serious and violent juvenile crime* (Office of Juvenile Justice and Delinquency Prevention No. NCJ- 161565). Washington, DC: U. S. Department of Justice.

Torbet, P., & Szymanski, L. (1998). *State legislative responses to violent juvenile crime: 1996–1997 update* (Office of Juvenile Justice and Delinquency Prevention). Washington, DC: U. S. Department of Justice.

Walker, S. (1994). *Sense and nonsense about crime and drugs a policy guide* (3rd ed.). Belmont, CA: Wadsworth.

Zimring, F. E. (1998). *American youth violence.* New York: Oxford University.

Chapter 1

History

Sheri Jenkins Keenan

While waiving juvenile offenders to the adult criminal courts continues to be a controversial subject, it is difficult to understand how this policy has developed without first understanding several key events. The first is the historical evolution of the treatment of children. Next are the events leading up to the formation of the first juvenile court in the United States. Third is the prevailing philosophy behind the juvenile justice system. Finally, there is the due process revolution that transformed the juvenile justice system into what we have today.

HISTORICAL PERSPECTIVE OF THE TREATMENT OF CHILDREN

From ancient times through medieval times, children were treated as property. Children were chattel to be disposed of at the whim of the family patriarch. Children could be bought, sold, kept living, left to die, or even killed. The child's fate was left to the family's patriarch; the oldest living blood-kin male (Mays & Winfree, 2000; Watson, 1970).

The first correctional institution for the control of juvenile delinquency in the United States was the New York House of Refuge (1825); however, specialized treatment of wayward juveniles has a much longer history (Bernard, 1992; Bilick, 2004; Howell, 1997; Krisberg, 2004; Pickett, 1969; Wines, 1970). Children have been committing delinquent acts since the beginning of time, and while approaches to dealing with such behaviors were not systematically codified until the nineteenth century, one can find early forms of punishment for juvenile delinquency. For example, the Biblical recommendation for responding to a stubborn and rebellious son is stoning.

> If any man has a stubborn and rebellious son who will not obey his father or his mother, and when they chastise him, he will not even listen to them, then his father and mother shall seize him, and bring him out to the elders of his city at the gateway of his hometown. They shall say to the elders of his city, "This son of ours is stubborn and rebellious, he will not obey us, he is a glutton and a drunkard." Then all the men of his city shall stone him to death; so you shall remove the evil from your midst, and all Israel will hear of it and fear. (Deuteronomy 21: 18–21)

Ancient Babylon

Approximately 4,000 years ago, around 1750 B.C., King Hammurabi of Babylon in Sumeria presided over the first state known to be governed by a written legal code. The Code of Hammurabi is one of the oldest known sets of written laws (Lawrence & Hemmens, 2008; Martin, 2005; Regoli & Hewitt, 2006). Hammurabi ruled Babylon from 1792 to 1750 B.C (Regoli & Hewitt, 2006). He created over 200 rules for the kingdom, each accompanied by an exact punishment (Regoli & Hewitt, 2006). Many of the rules prescribed severe penalties, applying the dictum "an eye for an eye" (Leviticus 24:19–20).

The Code of Hammurabi also incorporated complex provisions for marriage, fidelity, and family solidarity (Lawrence & Hemmens, 2008; Martin, 2005; Regoli & Hewitt, 2006). It did so by designating the husband at the unquestioned head of the household. Children were treated as little more than property. Children, defined during this time as the offspring from a freeman's wife, concubine, and slave, were under the father's control until emancipated by marriage (Martin, 2005). Children were an extension of their father. The father could hire out a child's labor. Children could be indentured to others for their father's debts, or he could sell them (Lawrence & Hemmens, 2008; Martin, 2005; Regoli & Hewitt, 2006). Girls could be given by fathers to serve the gods in temples, or given away as concubines, with no choice in the matter (Martin, 2005). Boys were required to be obedient and respectful to the father on pain of extreme physical punishment such as amputation (Martin, 2005). For example,

> If a son strikes his father, his hands shall be cut off (Rule 195).
>
> The code also established a special set of rules for adopted children. For instance,
>
> If an adopted child says to his father or mother "You are not my father or my mother," his tongue shall be cut off (Rule 192).
>
> In addition, the code goes on to say,
>
> If an adopted son returned to their biological parents then his eyes would be plucked out (Rule 193).

Juvenile delinquency was viewed as rebellion against the father, and the law brutally enforced respect for and fear of paternal authority (Lawrence & Hemmens, 2008; Martin, 2005; Regoli & Hewitt, 2006).

The Greeks

The Greek Empire covered the years between the sixth and third centuries (500–300 B.C.). Juvenile delinquency was considered to be a serious problem in Greek society. The Greek culture responded to delinquency by passing laws that held parents responsible for the behavior of their children. Scholars (Cox, Allen, Hanser & Conrad, 2008; Cherry, 1890; Martin, 2005; Regoli & Hewitt, 2006; Lawrence & Hemmens, 2008) suggest that these are likely the first parental liability laws; the first parent liability laws in the United States are found in the Massachusetts Stubborn Child Law of 1646 (Regoli & Hewitt, 2006).

The Romans

Roman law had a direct influence on modern European legal codes. Roman jurisprudence was derived from two sources: The Code of Justinian and the Twelve Tables. The Code of Justinian was a code of laws written during the reign of Justinian, Emperor of the Eastern Empire. It was originally promulgated in 529 B.C. and comprised twelve books. It became one of four compilations of Roman law known collectively as the Corpus Juris Civilis (Cox et al., 2008; Cherry, 1890; Martin, 2005).

The earliest known laws of the Roman people are comprised in the code of the Twelve Tables, which was compiled by the Decemvirs about the year 450 B.C. (Cox et al., 2008; Cherry, 1890; Martin, 2005). The Twelve Tables made it clear that children were criminally responsible for violations of law and were to be dealt with by the criminal justice system (Cox et al., 2008; Lawrence & Hemmens, 2008; Nyquist, 1960). Originally, children who were incapable of speech were spared under Roman law, but eventually, as the law came to reflect an increasing recognition of childhood, immunity was afforded to all children under the age of seven.

The Roman city-state embraced the philosophy that viewed children as having little-to-no social status; often lower than even the slaves (Mays & Winfree, 2000; Martin, 2005). This status was codified in the *patrai potestas* (Mays & Winfree, 2000; Martin, 2005), literally power of the father, a part of the paterfamilias doctrine, whereby the father was the head of the family. This legal dictum placed the child under the father's absolute control as long as the father lived, but the father could emancipate the child if he so wished. The Code in the Twelve Tables specified sanctions for children who were deformed or caught stealing, or who otherwise displeased their fathers (Ludwig, 1955; Martin, 2005). For example,

> Monstrous or deformed offspring may be put to death by the father.
>
> A father shall have the right of life and death over his son born in lawful marriage and shall also have the power to render him independent, after he has been sold three times.
>
> The father shall, during his whole life, have absolute power over his children. He may imprison his son, or scourge him, or keep him working in the fields in fetters, or put him to death, even if the son held the highest offices of state.

While the father was bound by practical limits as to what he could or would do to his children, the legal code remained largely unchanged until the fourth century. In 374 A.D., a law forbade the exposure of infants to the elements, a common method of disposing of unwanted children, mostly daughters. At about the same time, the writings of early Christian philosophers, including St. Augustine, helped quiet the *patria potestas* in favor of the more benevolent *paterna pietas*, or fatherly love (Martin, 2005; Mounteer, 1984). In spite of the changes in the fourth and fifth centuries, *patria potestas* remained a central theme in Roman law though its last great revision by the Byzantine emperor Justinian I in the sixth century (Jolowicz, 1957; Martin, 2005).

The collapse of the Roman Empire in the fifth century marked the beginning of the Middle Ages. The sociopolitical power of Christianity had evolved to the point that the belief in the immortal soul of all humans meant that children suffered less brutish treatment than in earlier times. Childhood was viewed as a time for inculcation of Christian beliefs (Martin, 2005; McLaughlin, 1975). The Roman Catholic Church even helped define the age of culpability for children; seven (Ozment, 1983). Moreover, during this period of growing church power in the affairs of society, the father's power declined.

Medieval life generally was nasty, brutish, and short (Hobbes, 1668). Given the growth of cities and the poor sanitary standards of the day, deadly diseases were rampant. Plague, smallpox, whooping cough, scarlet fever, diphtheria, and measles often took more lives than they spared, the children were at particular risk for dying (Thornton & Voigt, 1992). The parents love for a child was ill-advised in a time when so many died so young. As Aries (1962) has observed,

> In medieval society the idea of childhood did not exist; this is not to suggest that children were neglected, forsaken or despised. The idea of childhood is not to be confused with affection for children: it corresponds to an awareness of the particular nature of childhood, that particular nature which distinguishes the

> child from the adult, even the young adult. In medieval society this awareness was lacking. (Aries, 1962, p. 128)

Aries's (1962) conclusions have been criticized; however, it is important to observe that medieval Europe lacked separate institutions for the socialization of children (Binder, Gilbert & Dickson, 1988; Martin, 2005; Thornton & Voigt, 1992). Children learned their roles and expectations by wandering through the world of adults. They played adult games, performed adult jobs, dressed like adults, and basically led adult lives from a very early age (Mays & Winfree, 2000; Thornton & Voigt, 1992).

England

Roman and canon (church) law undoubtedly influenced early Anglo-Saxon common law; law based on custom or use, which emerged in England during the eleventh and twelfth centuries. The distinctions made between adult and juvenile offenders in England at this time are most significant. Under common law, children under the age of seven were presumed to be incapable of forming criminal intent and were not subject to criminal sanctions unless it could be demonstrated that they could distinguish right from wrong (Blackstone, 1803; Cox et al., 2008; Lawrence & Hemmens, 2008; Martin, 2005). Children over the age of fourteen were treated the same as adults.

Another important step in the history of juvenile justice occurred during the fifteenth century when chancery or equity courts were created by the King of England. Chancery courts, under the guidance of the king's chancellor, were created to consider petitions of those who were in need of special aid or intervention, such as women and children left in need of protection and aid by reason of divorce, death of a spouse, or abandonment (Cox et al., 2008; Lawrence & Hemmens, 2008; Martin, 2005). Through the chancery courts, the king exercised the right of *parens patriae* or parent of the country by enabling these courts to act *in loco parentis* or in the place of parents to provide necessary services for the benefit of women and children (Bynum & Thompson, 1992; Cox et al., 2008; Lawrence & Hemmens, 2008; Martin, 2005; Siegel & Welsh, 2009).

In the sixteenth and seventeenth centuries, life in Europe was in flux economically, religiously, and politically (Krisberg, 2004). First, the economy was transforming from a rural and agricultural society with its small towns into an urban and industrial society with its rapidly growing inhabitance, increasingly chaotic streets, and different racial and ethnic groups (Krisberg, 2004). Next, religious turmoil took the form of the reformation (Krisberg, 2004). Finally, political power was being concentrated in the hands of a few, thus creating a strong centralized government (Krisberg, 2004). The standard of living of the general population dropped sharply forcing mass migration to the cities. The workers and artisans of these cities believed that the growing migrant population would drive down work wages. In addition, these cities were also experiencing increasing crime rates (Krisberg, 2004).

To control the threat of this new "dangerous class" (Brace, 1872; Krisberg, 2004; Shelden, 2001), the leaders of these cities enacted laws to discourage migration: Elizabethan Statue of Artificers (1952) and poor laws (1601) (Cox et al., 2008; Rendleman, 1974). Both of these statues allowed children of poor families to be involuntarily separated from their parents and bound out as indentured servants; apprentice (Brace, 1872; Cox et al., 2008; Krisberg, 2004; Rendleman, 1974; Shelden, 2001). In addition, these statutes prevented new migrants from obtaining citizenship, restricting their membership in guilds, and often closing the city gates to them (Brace, 1872; Cox et.al., 2008; Krisberg, 2004; Shelden, 2001). Both statutes were based on the belief that the state has a primary interest in the welfare of children and the right to ensure such welfare (Cox et al., 2008). Vagrancy laws were also enacted to control and punish those who threatened the social order.

Urbanization continued despite all attempts to squash (Krisberg & Austin, 1993). Social institutions, such as the church, the community, and the family, began to weaken under the pressure of social change. Children were abandoned or released from traditional community restraints and groups of juveniles roamed the cities at night engaging in forms of deviance. (Krisberg, 2004; Sanders, 1970)

As the problem of urban poverty increased, the traditional ways of dealing with delinquent and destitute juveniles became strained. Some localities constructed institutions to control juveniles. The Bridewell (1555) in London is considered the first juvenile institution specifically designed to control juveniles (Brace, 1872; Krisberg, 2004; Sellin, 1944). In 1576, the English Parliament passed a law establishing similar institutions throughout England (Brace, 1872; Krisberg, 2004; Sellin, 1944). The most celebrated of these early institutions was the Amsterdam House of Corrections (1595) (Krisberg, 2004; Sellin, 1944). These houses of correction combined the principles of the poorhouse, the workhouse, and the penal institution (Garland, 1990). Juveniles were forced to work; thus developing habits of industriousness (Krisberg, 2004). The founders of such institutions hoped to provide a cheap source of labor to local industries, so many of the juveniles were hired out to private contractors (Krisberg, 2004).

The early houses of correction accepted all types of juveniles including the destitute, the infirmed, and the needy. In some cases, parents placed their children in these institutions (Krisberg, 1993, 2004; Shelden, 2001; Rusche & Kirchheimer, 1939). The French correctional institutions were called *hospitaux generaux*. Some authors (Krisberg, 2004; Shelden, 2001; Rusche

& Kirchheimer, 1939) argue that these early correctional institutions were solely motivated by economics. Rusche and Kirchheimer (1939) in their book, *Punishment and Social Structure*, argued, "The institution of the house of correction in such a society was not the result of brotherly love or of an official sense of obligation to the distressed. It was part of the development of capitalism" (p. 50).

The United States

The social, political, and economic dislocation taking place in Europe provided a major push toward colonization of the Americas. People immigrated to the new world for many reasons; some wanted to get rich, some wanted to escape political or religious oppression, and some simply had nothing to lose. These different motivations for immigrating to the new world influenced settlement patterns and were responsible for the varied forms of community life. For example, in the Massachusetts Bay Colony, the Puritans attempted to establish a deeply religious community. The Puritans brought whole families with them and making provisions for the care and control of juveniles. In contrast, the settlement of Virginia was tied to economic considerations. There were persistent labor shortages, and the need for labor prompted orders for juveniles to be sent over from Europe. Juveniles were sent over by Spirits. Spirits were the agents of merchants or ship owners (Lawrence & Hemmens, 2008), and persuaded juveniles to immigrate to America often promising tremendous wealth and happiness (Lawrence & Hemmens, 2008). The juveniles typically agreed to work a specific term, usually four years, in compensation for passage across the Atlantic and for services rendered during the trip (Krisberg, 2004; Lawrence & Hemmens, 2008). These agreements of service were then sold to colonist. Spirits were often accused of kidnapping, contractual fraud, and deception (Krisberg, 2004; Lawrence & Hemmens, 2008).

Other children coming to the Americas were clearly coerced. It became an integral part of penal practice in the early part of the eighteenth century to transport prisoners to colonial area. Juveniles held in the overcrowded Bridewells and poorhouses of England were brought to the Americans as indentured servants, and after working a specified number of years as servants or laborers, the children were able to win their freedom (Krisberg, 2004). In the early 1600s, the colony of Virginia and England formulated an agreement for the shipment of orphans and destitute children from England (Durant & Knottnerus, 1999; Krisberg & Austin, 1993; Stampp, 1956; Yetman, 1970). Africans made their first appearance in the Virginia Colony in 1619 (Durant & Knottnerus, 1999; Stampp, 1956; Yetman, 1970). According to Yetman (2000), studies conducted on slavery neglect to mention the fact that most slaves were children. Slave traders thought children would bring higher prices (Durant & Knottnerus, 1999; Stampp, 1956; Yetman, 1970, 2000). Children were always a high proportion of the total slave population, because slave owners encouraged their slave to have children; thus, increased slave owners capital (Durant & Knottnerus, 1999; Krisberg, 2004; Stampp, 1956; Yetman, 1970, 2000). African babies were seen as a commodity to be exploited similarly to that of land, animals, and natural resources (Durant & Knottnerus, 1999; Stampp, 1956; Yetman, 1970, 2000).

In 1609, officials of the Virginia Company were authorized to kidnap Native American children (Krisberg, 2004; Krisberg & Austin, 1993). The stolen children were to be trained in the religion, language, and customs of the colonists (Krisberg, 2004). The early Native American schools resembled penal institutions; emphasis on work, Bible study, and religious worship (Krisberg, 2004).

In the early years of colonization, family control was the dominant model for disciplining children. The family was also the central unit of economic production. Even in situations where children were apprenticed or indentured, the family still served as the model for discipline. The dominant form of poor relief at this time was placing the needy with other families in the community (Krisberg, 2004; Krisberg & Austin, 1993; Rothman, 1971). A tradition of family government evolved in which the father was empowered with absolute authority over all affairs of the family (Krisberg and Austin, 1993). Wives and children were expected to obey the family patriarch.

The idea of family government was supported and defended in a number of colonial laws (Krisberg & Austin, 1993). The earliest laws concerning juvenile delinquency prescribed the death penalty for children who disobeyed their parents (Bilick, 2004; Hawes, 1971; Hess, 2010; Krisberg, 2004). The family was the central economic unit of colonial America. Home-based industry took place on the family farm or in a home workshop. Children were considered an important source of family income. So much so, that the decision of the father as to where the child was to be apprenticed was vitally important not only for the family, but the child's future as well (Krisberg, 2004; Krisberg & Austin, 1993; Lawrence & Hemmens, 2008). The apprenticeship system was to be the steppingstone into a skilled craft, but this was only for children of the privileged classes. Children of poor families were bound out as indentured servants. The term of apprenticeship was generally seven years. The child was expected to regard his master with the same obedience due their natural parents (Krisberg, 2004). The master was responsible for the education and training of the young apprentice and he acted in *loco parentis*. *Loco Parentis* is a Latin term meaning acting in the place of the parent (Oran, 2000). By acting in loco parentis, the master was assuming complete responsibility for the child's welfare. Apprenticeships were voluntary for the wealthier juveniles; however, for the wayward or destitute juveniles, they were unavoidable. The use of compulsory apprenticeship was an important form of social control exercised by cities officials upon juveniles perceived as troublesome (Bremner, 1970; Krisberg, 2004).

The industrial revolution in the United States began at the end of the eighteenth century. The economy was transforming from a rural agricultural society into an urban industrial society. The industrial revolution forced family units from the family farm into large cities for survival. Child labor in industrial settings replaced the apprenticeship system and family ties weakened because workdays were long (Krisberg, 2004; Krisberg & Austin, 1993). As migration, emigration and industrialization continued, the streets of these large cities became chaotic, and conditions of poverty began to spread. As economic instability increased, the traditional forms of social control decreased and Americans began to fear the growth of the "dangerous class" (Brace, 1872; Krisberg, 2004; Shelden, 2001).

THE CREATION OF JUVENILE JUSTICE

Before the 1800s, the United States had no juvenile justice system (Empey, 1978; Elton & Roybal, 2003; Finestone, 1976; Houston & Barton, 2005; Howell, 1997; National Research Council Staff, 2000; Schwartz, 1989). Criminal cases involving juveniles were processed through the adult criminal courts (Finestone, 1976; Howell, 1997; Schwartz, 1989; Thornton & Voigt, 1992). Juveniles who were convicted of crimes were subject to the same sanctions as adults, were incarcerated in facilities with adults, and were even executed like adults (Siegel & Welsh, 2009; Thornton & Voigt, 1992). There is no record of the numbers of juveniles confined in adult prisons in the United States either during the colonial era or during the American Industrial Revolution.

As alluded to before, the United States inherited from England and other European countries a disregard for children, and it was not until the end of the Middle Ages that a handful of moral philosophers in Europe began to question the customary treatment of children (Empey, 1978; Finestone, 1976; Krisberg, 2004). Over a period of the next two or three centuries, the age-old tendencies—infanticide, abandonment, wet nursing, swaddling, economic and sexual exploitation of children—were replaced with a concern for their moral welfare (Empey, 1978; Finestone, 1976; Krisberg, 2004; Schwartz, 1989). Parental care for children became a sacred duty. School attendance laws replaced the apprenticeship system as the second most important child rearing institution (Empey, 1978; Finestone, 1976; Schwartz, 1989). Childhood became a transitional period in which protection from adult activities became the norm. It is out of this process that the modern concepts of childhood, adulthood, and old age grew. Childhood is a concept stressing the idea that children have value in their own right and that because of their innocence they require a careful preparation from the harshness and sinfulness of an adult world (Empey, 1978; Finestone, 1976; Schwartz, 1989). Furthermore, it was only after all of these things occurred, only after childhood became a special status in the life cycle, that the establishment of special courts and incarceration facilities occurred, along with Kindergarten, child labor laws, mandatory education, school lunches, and vocational education; all aimed at enhancing optimal child development in the industrial city (National Research Council Staff, 2000). It was not until the beginning of the twentieth century and the creation of the juvenile court that these terms were developed and used in delinquency prevention and control policies (Empey, 1978; Finestone, 1976; Howell, 1997; Schwartz, 1989).

There were three events that led to the creation of correctional institutions especially for juveniles; the emergence of pauperism, the development of prisons (e.g., the creation of Auburn [New York] State Prison in 1819; Sing Sing [Ossining, New York] in 1825; and Wethersfield [Connecticut] State Prison in 1827; and the Eastern State Penitentiary [Philadelphia] in 1829), and the work of the "gentleman reformers" (Finestone, 1976) and the "child savers" (Platt, 1969) (Bernard, 1992; Howell, 1997; Pickett, 1969; Platt, 1969; Siegel & Welsh, 2009).

The term "juvenile delinquency" was first used two hundred years ago (Empey, 1978; Bernard, 1992) in a report examining the increase of juvenile delinquency which came out in London in 1816 (Bernard, 1992; Sanders, 1970). The term 'juvenile delinquency' describes minors who have committed an offense punishable by criminal processes, but who are under the statutory age for criminal responsibility (Griffin, Addie, Adams, & Firestine, 2011). When a juvenile commits a criminal act, it is considered an act of juvenile delinquency (Bernard, 1992; Griffin et al., 2011).

During the 1800s in the United States, society was being led by a group of moralist advocates whom Finestone (1976) called "gentleman reformers." These gentlemen reformers were largely white Anglo-Saxon Protestants, although a few were Quakers, middle- to upper-class, cosmopolitan men who kept up with reforms abroad (Finestone, 1976; Howell, 1997; Pickett, 1969). They were a very active group guided by the eighteenth-century Enlightenment. They were led by humanitarian, idealism, moralism, and rationalism. Having concluded that pauperism or poverty undermined society, the gentleman reformers set out to eliminate its effects (Finestone, 1976; Howell, 1997; Pickett, 1969).

In 1817, a meeting was convened by prominent New Yorkers to consider cures for pauperism and crime (Howell, 1997). This meeting led to the formation of the Society for the Prevention of Pauperism in New York City

(Howell, 1997; Siegel & Welsh, 2009). Although they primarily concerned themselves with shutting down taverns, brothels, and gambling parlors, they were also concerned that the moral training of children of the lower classes (Siegel & Welsh, 2009). The Society for the Prevention of Pauperism was shocked to find children confined with thieves, prostitutes, and lunatics in unsanitary quarters (Dean & Reppucci, 1974). In 1822, the Society for the Prevention of Pauperism called public attention to the corruption of children by locking them up with adult criminals. The society called for the rescue of children from a future of crime and degradation (Howell, 1997). In 1823, the Society for the Prevention of Pauperism reconstituted itself as the Society for the Reformation of Juvenile Delinquents, as juveniles became its target for reform (Bernard, 1992; Finestone, 1976; Howell, 1997).

House of Refuge

The idea of creating the House of Refuge in New York City did not happen overnight. The Reverend John Stanford raised the subject as early as 1815, and the idea had shifted back and forth between Stanford and the city government for almost a decade (Pickett, 1969). Stanford was angry at the number of juveniles in the city's prisons. For many years, he had urged the city authorities to remove the juveniles from the city's prisons, and place them in separate institution (Pickett, 1969). Stanford developed a plan for an asylum which would house two types of juveniles: "little wanderers" and "criminals" (Pickett, 1969, p. 21). "Little Wanderers" (Pickett, 1969, p. 21) were juveniles who had been either abandoned or who had run away from their parents. The other part of the asylum would house juveniles who had been tried and convicted in the courts; criminals (Pickett, 1969). Stanford suggested work, education, and religion as the prime means to alter deviant behavior (Pickett, 1969). Part of the juvenile's time would be spent in learning manufacturing skills while the remainder would be spent in learning elementary academic subjects. Stanford gave a very high priority to religion (Pickett, 1969). Stanford's idea was rejected by those in power; later, the idea was put forward successfully by others who had more influence (Pickett, 1969).

Ten years later, members of the Society for the Reformation of Juvenile Delinquents advocated that the laws must change in order to address societal conditions caused by the transformation of America from a rural and agricultural society with its small towns into an urban and industrial society with its rapidly growing inhabitance, increasingly chaotic streets, and different racial and ethnic groups (Krisberg, 2004; Tanenhaus, 2000). The view of societal conditions being the potential cause of criminal behavior is consistent with the development of positive criminology during the 1800s and the Progressive movement (Howell, 1997; Empey, 1978; Finestone, 1976;

Schwartz, 1989; Siegel & Welsh, 2009). Positive criminology sought to determine the impact of outside forces such as social, economic, biological, and psychological forces on individual behavior (Adler, Mueller & Laufer, 1995; Barlow, 1990; Cao, 2004; Cullen & Agnew, 2006; Siegel, 2004; Vold, Bernard & Snipes, 1998). In addition, this period also witnessed growing interest in the scientific approach to the social problems and in the belief that the social sciences would provide answers to these problems. This influenced reformers to advocate for nonpunitive measures and an emphasis on individualized diagnosis and treatment of juveniles based on the medical mode, a concept more popularly known as the rehabilitative ideal (Schwartz, 1989). These developments lead to the belief that in order to reduce crime, the law had to grant states the necessary powers to address these societal conditions (Tanenhaus, 2000).

As a result of this new focus and the passage of a law (Fox, 1996) by the New York legislature in 1824 authorizing the opening of the New York House of Refuge, the New York City Mayor, Cadwallader D. Colden (1769–1834), John Griscom (1774–1852), a professor of chemistry and natural philosophy and eventually principal of New York City's Chief secondary school, Thomas Eddy (1757–1827), a banker, Hugh Maxwell, James W. Gerard, and the Society for the Reformation of Juvenile Delinquents developed and established the New York House of Refuge in 1825 (Bernard, 1992; Hawes, 1971; Howell, 1997; Krisberg, 2004; Mennel, 1973; Pickett, 1969; Thornton & Voigt, 1992; Wines, 1970). The Society for the Reformation of Juvenile Delinquents believed that there were three possible causes of pauperism and crime: weak and criminal parents, the temptations of the street, and the weakness of the juvenile's moral nature (Bernard, 1992; Howell, 1997; Pickett, 1969; Platt, 1969). The Society believed that the House of Refuge addressed all three of these problems by removing the children from their parents and the street and placing them in the House of Refuge to rehabilitate their weak moral natures (Bernard, 1992; Empey, 1978; Finestone, 1976; Howell, 1997; Pickett, 1969; Platt, 1969; Schwartz, 1989; Thornton & Voigt, 1992). These reformers believed that the House of Refuge would successfully cure delinquency.

The majority of the children committed to the new House of Refuge were status offenders. Juveniles were placed in the House of Refuge by court order, and often times over the parents' objections. The juveniles' length of stay depended on need, age, and skill (Siegel & Welsh, 2009). Emphasis was placed on work, education, and morality. The House of Refuge became family substitutes for juveniles who were defined as a problem: the runaways, the disobedient, the defiant and the vagrant, all of whom were in danger of falling prey to lose women, taverns, gambling halls, and the theater (Howell, 1997). Only those who could still be rescued were sent to the House of Refuge by the court (Howell, 1997). Major juvenile offenders were left in the adult criminal system (Howell, 1997), thus creating an unspoken juvenile transfer mechanism from the beginning.

Critics of the House of Refuge complained that the institution was run like a prison, that is, the Auburn congregate model and the Elmira Reformatory for Adults, with strict discipline, mixed education, income-generating labor, and absolute separation of the genders (Bernard, 1992; Howell, 1997; Siegel & Welsh, 2009). Despite the harsh conditions and the high rates of running away, the (Ryerson, 1978) House of Refuge concept quickly spread to other cities; Boston (1826) and Philadelphia (1828).

In Boston, Mayor Josiah Quincy (1772–1864) was responsible for founding the local house of reformation. His work was supported by his successors, notably Theodor Lyman, Jr. (1792–1849), mayor of Boston from 1831 to 1835 (Mennel, 1973). The Philadelphia House of Refuge resulted from the efforts of a group of reformers whose plans were given shape by Isaac Collins, who moved from New York to Philadelphia in 1828. Among the managers of the Philadelphia Refuge was Robert Vaux (1786–1836), a leader of the Philadelphia Society for Alleviating the Miseries of the Public Prisons, Alexander Henry (1766–1847), the first president of the American Sunday School Union, and Paul Beck, Jr., Thomas P. Cope, and Robert Ralston, all of whom were active in the American Sunday School Union. John Sergeant (1779–1852), a congressman and advocate of the United States Bank, was the first president of the refuge. Sarah Grimke (1792–1873), an abolitionist and feminist, served on the Ladies Committee.

Later, these juvenile facilities were called reform schools and a number of preventive agencies were created (Mennel, 1973). The most prominent of these preventive agencies was the Children's Mission to the Children of the Destitute (1849), the Five Points Mission (1850), the New York Juvenile Asylum (1851), and the New York Children's Aid Society (1853) (Mennel, 1973). When the name reform schools became objectionable, the school idea was given prominence, and they came to be called industrial or training schools (Dean & Reppucci, 1974; Howell, 1997; Mennel, 1973). In 1835, a farm-school was opened for orphans and poor children on Thompson's Island in the harbor of Boston (Wines, 1970). The state reform school was established at Westborough, Massachusetts, in 1847, and eight years later in 1855, the first girls' reformatory was founded at Lancaster, Massachusetts (Wines, 1970).

Placing Out

As an alternative to secure correctional facilities, New York philanthropist Charles Loring Brace helped develop the Children's Aid Society (1853)

(Holt, 1992; Siegel & Welsh, 2009). Brace's idea for dealing with juvenile delinquents was to rescue them from the harsh conditions of the street and provide them with temporary shelter. Upon realizing that the number of children in need was too great, Brace created what he called his placing-out plan (Holt, 1992; Siegel & Welsh, 2009). The placing-out plan comprised sending juveniles to western families where they could live and be cared for. Juveniles were placed on orphan trains, which made preannounced stops in western communities. Families wishing to take in children would meet the train, be introduced to the juveniles, and then leave with one of them. Brace's plan was activated in 1854 and shortly became the norm. After 1854 and the placing-out plan, the House of Refuge became nothing more than holding stations for poor children until they could be placed on trains heading west to be indentured out for service until they reached their twenty-first birthdays (Holt, 1992; Siegel & Welsh, 2009). The parents of these juveniles were not told where the child had ended up, nor were they allowed to have any further contact with the child since they were usually seen as the original source of the problem (Bernard, 1992; Holt, 1992). Many children were never heard from again. Many of the juveniles sent out west to their new homes became problems due to the terrible conditions under which they lived. By 1930, opposition to Brace's placing-out plan, the negative effects of the economic depression, and many western states passing laws forbidding the practice, brought an end to the orphan trains (Bernard, 1992; Holt, 1992; Siegel & Welsh, 2009).

As stated before, the idea of the House of Refuge spread quickly; New York (1825), Boston (1826), Philadelphia (1828), and subsequently in other cities. With the development of the Houses of Refuge came laws enacted to justify their existence and more importantly the actions of their administrators. In 1831, the case of *Commonwealth v M'Keagy* became one of the first to question the state's power to commit juveniles to reform schools (Bilick, 2004; *Commonwealth v. M'Keagy* 1 Ashmead (PA) 248 (1831); Gold, 2007).

The case involved a Pennsylvania boy, Lewis L. Joseph. Joseph had been committed to the Philadelphia House of Refuge on the testimony of his father for being an idle and disorderly person. Joseph's attorney filed a petition for a writ of *habeas corpus* and the Court of Common Pleas ordered Joseph released. The court found that Joseph had broken no law. While allowing the reform school to retain the power to commit juveniles, the court ruled that the reasons for commitment must be based on law. Idleness, the court declared, was not a good enough reason to deprive a juvenile of freedom. While affirming the right of the state, the court found in this instance, the juvenile's commitment was wrong.

In the mid-1800s, the question of whether parental rights were violated by involuntary refuge commitments was reviewed in *Ex parte Crouse* (1838)

(Bilick, 2004). Mary Ann Crouse was a poor child whose only crime was growing up poor and being in danger of becoming a pauper. Mary Ann's mother brought her into the court and committed her to the House of Refuge against her father's wishes. Crouse's father objected to this involuntary commitment of his daughter and filed a writ of *habeus corpus*. Mary Ann's father raised the issue that committing his daughter for being poor was punishment without a crime. In 1838, the Pennsylvania Supreme Court rejected the father's arguments. The Court held that sending Mary Ann to the House of Refuge was legal. The Court held that Mary Ann was being helped, not punished, viewed the House of Refuge as a charitable school, not a prison, and that the House of Refuge was going to save Mary Ann from the terrible fate of being a pauper. The Crouse case affirmed the right of the state and the concept of *parens patriae*; the state as parent, allowing the state, acting in the best interests of the child to pick up and hold juveniles. It was not until the case of Daniel O'Connell, forty-five years later, that issues raised in the Mary Ann Crouse case would be revisited.

Massachusetts built the first state-supported institutions for juveniles; the Lyman School for Boys in Westborough in 1847, and the School for Girls in Lancaster in 1854 (Howell, 1997). These reform schools were modeled after the earlier Houses of Refuge, European boarding schools, and Sunday Schools that provided moral and academic instruction as well as the adult prison in New York, Pennsylvania, and Massachusetts (Miller & Ohlin, 1985). The Chicago Reform School was established in 1856 (Howell, 1997). This school housed boys convicted of any noncapital offense, including juveniles convicted in adult criminal courts (Howell, 1997). Emphasis was placed on small facilities. Juveniles were to be protected, not punished for their actions. Also, emphasis was placed on creating a family life for these juveniles (Fox, 1970). By the middle of the nineteenth century, establishment of correctional institutions for poor, wayward, and delinquent juveniles were well established.

Throughout the nineteenth century, juvenile reform schools were involved in repeated scandals, overcrowding, abusive discipline, reforms and renewed regimentation (Bremner, 1970; Hawes, 1971; Howell, 1997; Holl, 1971; Mennel, 1973; Pickett, 1969; Platt, 1969; Schlossman, 1977). Family style cottages in rural setting that resembled school campuses, patterned after the Elmira New York reformatory for adults emerged in the 1850s and 1860s. These family style cottage settings were also characterized by extreme disciplinary measures, excessive regimentation, and overcrowding. Although treatment was the goal, the custodial needs of the juvenile institutions prevailed, dominated by maintenance of order and discipline as preconditions for treatment (Miller & Ohlin, 1985).

Juvenile reform schools did not become what the reformers envisioned. Rather than an institution of first resort, juvenile reformatories became an institution of last resort. They had turned into prisons, providing custody rather than treatment. Gradually, they became acceptable as the choice for confinement of lower-class and minority juveniles (Howell, 1997). In 1860, the administration of juvenile facilities became the purview of the state and local governments. By 1876, there were fifty-one refuges or reform schools in the United States. Problems persisted and grew. Repeated violence in the reformatories became public knowledge and a series of investigations was conducted (Wines, 1970) that produced further efforts to improve juvenile reform schools.

In another important case, *People v. Turner* (1870), the right of the state to intervene in the lives of juveniles was challenged again. Daniel O'Connell, like Mary Ann Crouse, was placed in the Chicago House of Refuge until his twenty-first birthday not for committing any criminal offense other than being in danger of growing up poor. O'Connell's parents, like Crouse's father objected, and the Illinois Supreme Court ordered O'Connell released. The Illinois Supreme Court held that O'Connell was being punished. The Court weighted the harsh conditions of the House of Refuge to the good intentions of O'Connell's parents, and rejected the states' rights under the *parens patriae* doctrine.

People v. Turner (1870) was seen as an obstacle to the efforts of reformers to help and control juveniles. The court's ruling led reformers in Chicago to consider other mechanism by which their aims might be achieved. There were several other court decisions that questioned the lack of procedural safeguards and the quasi-penal character of juvenile institutions, including the *State v. Ray* (1886), and *Ex parte Becknell* (1897).

Society for the Prevention of Cruelty to Children

In 1874, New York City established the first Society for the Prevention of Cruelty to Children. This organization was given the power to remove children from their homes and arrest anyone who interfered, and assisted the court in making placement decisions. They also assisted the state legislature in passing statues protecting children from cruelty and neglect at home and at school (Fox, 1996; Gordon, 1988; Pleck, 1987, 1989; Siegel & Welsh, 2009). By 1890, the society controlled the intake and disposition of an annual average of 15,000 poor and neglected children (Fox, 1996; Gordon, 1988; Pleck, 1987; 1989; Siegel and Welsh, 2009). By 1900, there were three hundred such societies in the United States (Fox, 1996; Gordon, 1988; Pleck, 1987, 1989; Siegel & Welsh, 2009).

The First Juvenile Court

The first juvenile court was established seventy-five years after the New York House of Refuge was opened in 1825. The Illinois Juvenile Court Act of 1899 established the nation's first independent juvenile court (Bernard, 1992; Bilick, 2004; Davis, 1979; Fox, 1996; Houston & Barton, 2005; Howell, 1997; Ryerson, 1978; Schwartz, 1989; Siegel & Welch, 2009). The first juvenile court was created in Chicago, Illinois, in 1899 and established juvenile delinquency as a legal concept. The court's jurisdiction covered all manner of juveniles be they delinquent, dependent, or neglected. Additionally, the use of probation was established as the primary way of monitoring the wayward juvenile (Ryerson, 1978; Siegel & Welsh, 2009). The hallmark of the new juvenile courts was relatively simple; children, even children who broke the law, differ from adults (Bernard, 1992; Howell, 1997; Ryerson, 1978; Schwartz, 1989). They required not only separate but different treatment before the law (Bernard, 1992; Bilick, 2004; Howell, 1997; Ryerson, 1978; Schwartz, 1989; Siegel & Welch, 2009). The state acting through this new juvenile court must treat juveniles, not as responsible moral agents subject to the condemnation of the community, but as wards in need of care (Bernard, 1992; Finestone, 1976; Howell, 1997; Ryerson, 1978; Schwartz, 1989). The Illinois legislature decided that this special court for juveniles should be of civil jurisdiction, with flexible procedures adapted to diagnosing and preventing as well as to curing delinquency (Bernard, 1992; Ryerson, 1978).

The new juvenile court was founded on the concept of *parens patriae;* the state as parent, with the idea of individualized justice. The court's process was paternalistic rather than adversarial. The traditional rights afforded to adults were not in effect due to the specialized nature of the juvenile and their special needs (Moore & Wakeling, 1997; Siegel & Welsh, 2009)

Following the passage of the Illinois Juvenile Court Act (1899), and drawing on Chicago's juvenile court model, similar legislation was enacted and juvenile courts established throughout the nation. By 1912, twenty-two states had passed juvenile court laws, and by 1925, all but two states had done so (Bernard, 1992; Krisberg & Austin, 1993; Myers, 2005; Siegel & Welsh, 2009; Thomas & Bilchik, 1985). In 1945, Wyoming became the last state to establish a juvenile court (Binder, Geis & Dickson, 2001; Myers, 2005).

As juvenile courts were being established throughout the country, they all held to the same basic principle; juveniles are different than adults and should not be held to the same standards of accountability or have the same constitutional rights as adults. The major functions of the juvenile justice system were to prevent juvenile crime and to rehabilitate juvenile offenders. The roles of the judge and probation staff were to diagnose the juvenile's condition and prescribe programs to rehabilitate the juvenile.

Pennsylvania was one of a large number of states that quickly followed in establishing its own juvenile court. In 1905, a decision by the Pennsylvania Supreme Court in the case of Frank Fisher reflected the optimistic way in which juvenile courts were viewed in the early 1900s (Bernard, 1992; Myers, 2005).

Frank Fisher was a fourteen-year-old boy who had been indicted for larceny in Philadelphia. His case was sent to this newly established juvenile court. He was sent to the same House of Refuge that had received Mary Ann Crouse sixty years earlier. Like Mary Ann Crouse's and Daniel O'Connell's father, Fisher's father objected and filed a write of *habeus corpus* in an attempt to obtain Fisher's release. Fisher has been charged with, not convicted of larceny, a criminal offense, so the "no punishment without a crime" issue raised in the *Crouse* and *O'Connell* cases did not apply. But a closely related principle was that, when a crime was committed, the punishment should be proportionate to the seriousness of the offense. Fisher had committed a minor offense but could be held in the House of Refuge until his twenty-first birthday, a total of seven years. This was much longer than he would have received in adult criminal court and seemed disproportionate to the seriousness of his offense.

The case went to the Pennsylvania Supreme Court, which had also heard the Mary Ann Crouse case sixty years earlier. As it did before, it rejected the arguments of Fisher's father. The court's rationale contained all of the same essential points found in the earlier *Crouse* decision. First, the court asserted that Fisher was being helped, not punished, by being confined in the Philadelphia House of Refuge. Second, the court focused on the good intentions of the state, especially in comparison to the poor actual performance of Fisher's parents. Third, the court argued that helping Fisher was legal because of the *parens patriae* power of the state. Finally, because Fisher was being helped and not punished, the court held that Fisher had no need for due process protections (Bernard, 1992; Krisberg & Austin, 1993; Myers, 2005).

By the 1920s, noncriminal or status offenses were added to the jurisdiction of juvenile court systems (Odem & Schlossman, 1991). Programs of all kinds, including individualized counseling and institutional care, were used to cure juvenile delinquency.

By the mid-1920s, juvenile courts existed in nearly every jurisdiction of every state (Fox, 1996); however, the implementation of these juvenile courts was not uniform (Fox, 1996). Some jurisdictions established elaborate juvenile court systems with trained juvenile court judges, probation departments, and numerous services, while others had non-lawyers and untrained probation personnel. In 1926, a United States Children's Bureau survey found that only 16 percent of these new juvenile courts held separate calendars for juvenile cases, had officially established probation services, and recorded social information about the children coming through the courts (Fox, 1996). It was also reported that five out of six of these courts in the United States failed to meet the minimum standards of the Children's Bureau (Fox, 1996).

THE DUE PROCESS REVOLUTION

From its inception through the 1960s, the juvenile court system denied due process rights available to adult offenders. These due process rights included the following: representation by counsel, jury trial, freedom from self-incrimination, and freedom from unreasonable search and seizure. The policies and practices of the juvenile court went unchallenged for the first sixty-seven years following its origin and development. The stated purpose of the juvenile court was for treatment rather than punishment. It resembled an informal civil proceeding more than a criminal trial, and the most severe sanctions for adjudicated delinquents were less than one year in a residential facility. This began to change in the 1960s (Bartollas & Miller, 2008; Bernard, 1992; Bilick, 2004; Champion & Mays, 1991; Davis, 1979; Elrod & Ryder, 2005; Gold, 2007; Houston & Barton, 2005; Ketcham & Paulsen, 1967; National Research Council Staff, 2000; Siegel & Tracy, 2008; Taylor, Fritsch & Caeti, 2007; Thornton & Voigt, 1992). *Kent v. United States, 383 U.S. 541 (1966).*

Kent v. United States (1966) was the first juvenile case to be heard by the United States Supreme Court. The *Crouse* (1938) and *Fisher* (1905) cases had gone to the Pennsylvania Supreme Court and *O'Connell* (1870) had gone to the Illinois Supreme Court. The acceptance of this case by the U.S. Supreme Court revealed its intention to apply constitutional protections to the juvenile court process and by the time *Breed v. Jones* (1975) was handed down juveniles enjoyed a majority of the due process rights adults have in adult criminal court.

In 1959, fourteen-year-old Morris A. Kent, Jr. was arrested and charged with several housebreakings and an attempted purse snatching. He was placed on probation and returned to the custody of his mother. Juvenile court officials interviewed Kent from time to time during the probation period and accumulated a social service file.

On September 2, 1961, Kent, now sixteen, broke into a woman's apartment, raped her, and stole her wallet. Upon being apprehended, Kent was interrogated from about 3:00 p.m. to 10:00 p.m. and then all the next day by police officers. Kent admitted his involvement in the offenses. The record did not show when his mother became aware that Kent was in custody but shortly after 2:00 p.m. on September 6, 1961, the day following Kent's apprehension, she retained counsel.

There were two decisions that had been handed down by the Court of Appeals between Kent's crime and trial. The *Watkins* (1964) decision ruled that a juvenile's lawyer should have access to social service files in waiver cases (*Watkins v. United States*, 343 F.2d 278, 282 (1964)), and the *Black* decision in 1965 held a juvenile was entitled to a lawyer in a waiver hearing

(*Black v. United States*, 355 F.2d. 104, (1965)). The United States Supreme Court affirmed these two lower court decisions.

In *Kent v. United States*, 383 U.S. 541 (1966), the U.S. Supreme Court ruled that the waiver without a hearing was invalid, and that Kent's attorney should have had access to all records involved in the waiver, along with a written statement of the reasons for the waiver. *Kent* is significant because it was the first Supreme Court case to modify the long standing belief that juveniles did not require the same due process protections as adults, because the intent of the juvenile court was treatment, not punishment. The majority opinion of the court noted that juveniles may receive the "worst of both worlds," "neither the protection accorded to adults nor the solicitous care and regenerative treatment postulated for children" (383 U.S. 541 (1966)). This decision served notice that the U. S. Supreme Court would consider cases involving the juvenile justice system.

In re Gault, 387 U.S. 1, S.Ct. 1428 (1967)

Gerald Gault, a fifteen-year-old boy who lived in Gila County, Arizona, had been on probation for about three months for being in the company of another boy who had stolen a wallet from a purse. On June 8, 1964, he and his friend Ronald Lewis called their neighbor, Mrs. Cook, and asked her, "Do you give any?" (387 U.S. 1, S.Ct. 1428 (1967)) "Are your cherries ripe today?"(387 U.S. 1, S.Ct. 1428 (1967)) and "Do you have big bombers?" (387 U.S. 1, S.Ct. 1428 (1967)), Mrs. Cook called the sheriff, who arrested the boys and placed them in detention. Gault's parents were not notified until the next day. At his court hearing, Gault was not represented by counsel, no record was kept, the victim was not present, and no evidence was presented regarding the charge. The judge stated that Gault admitted making the obscene remarks, whereas the Gaults said that Gerald only admitted dialing the phone. The judge said he would take it under advisement and Gault was released from detention two or three day later until a new hearing could be held.

A second hearing was held on June 15, 1964, with both Gault's mother and father attending. No record was kept of the hearing and Mrs. Cook did not appear. Mrs. Gault asked that Mrs. Cook identify which boy made the remakes, but the judge said it was not necessary. The judge then committed Gault to the State Industrial School for Boys until his twenty-first birthday; six years. The Gaults then retained a lawyer, who filed a writ of *habeas corpus*, demanding that the state justify holding Gault.

On appeal, the U.S. Supreme Court found that Gault's constitutional due process rights had been violated; it ruled that in hearings that could result in commitment to an institution, juveniles have the right to notice and counsel, to question witnesses, and to protection against self-incrimination (387 U.S. 1, S.Ct. 1428 (1967)).

The *Gault* (1967) case is the fourth of an alternating series of cases that began with Mary Ann Crouse in 1838. The crucial element of each decision is whether the U.S. Supreme Court focused on the good intentions or actual performance of the juvenile justice system. The *Crouse* (1838) case was heard thirteen years after the founding of the first juvenile institution and the Court was still optimistic about how well those institutions would work. The *O'Connell* (1870) case was heard thirty years later when the actual performance of the juvenile institutions was much more apparent. The optimism was renewed by the establishment of the first juvenile court in 1899 and was reflected in the *Fisher* (1905) case six years later. Sixty-two years later, the *Gault* (1967) decision affirmed an awareness of the failures of juvenile court system.

In re Winship, 387 U.S. 358 (1970)

In 1967, Samuel Winship, age twelve, was accused of stealing $112.00 from a purse in a furniture store in the Bronx. A store employee stated that Winship was seen running from the store just before the money was reported missing, but others in the store disputed that account, noting that the employee was not in a position to see the money actually being taken. At the juvenile court hearing, the judge agreed with Winship's attorney that there was some reasonable doubt of Winship's guilt, but New York juvenile courts, like those in most states, operated under the civil law standard of preponderance of evidence. Winship was adjudicated delinquent and committed to a New York training school for an initial period of eighteen months, subject to annual extensions for up to six years. Winship's attorney appealed the case on the issue of the burden of proof required in juvenile court. The U.S. Supreme Court ruled that the standard of evidence for adjudication of delinquency should be "proof beyond reasonable doubt" (387 U.S. 358 (1970)).

The legal issue in this case was whether proof beyond a reasonable doubt is among the essentials of due process and fair treatment required during the adjudicatory stage when a juvenile is charged with an act, which would constitute a crime if committed by an adult. The Supreme Court held that the same proof required for adults in their trials, should be the standard for juveniles in their adjudication proceedings for delinquent offenses. Status offenses maintained the preponderance of the evidence standard. Two years later, the Supreme Court made the *Winship* (1970) decision retroactive. Juveniles who had been adjudicated on a preponderance of the evidence would either have to be released from institutions or re-adjudicated by evidence that was beyond a reasonable doubt. This was unusually because normally decisions only apply after they are announced. This unusual move indicated how important the *Winship* (1970) decision was. The beyond-a-reasonable-doubt standard is used to assure that when the court finds that someone has committed a criminal act, that finding is accurate. Adjudications based on a preponderance of the evidence were held to be not accurate enough to warrant continuing to keep an individual in an institution. This same focus on accurate fact-finding reappears in the next case, where it involved the right to a jury trial.

McKeiver v. Pennsylvania, 403 U.S. 528 (1971)

In 1968, Joseph McKeiver, age sixteen of Philadelphia was charged with robbery, larceny, and receiving stolen goods. These three felony charges arose from an incident in which McKeiver and twenty plus other juveniles chased three younger teenagers and took twenty-five cents from them. McKeiver had never been arrested, was doing well in school, and was gainfully employed. The testimony of two of the three witnesses against him was described by the juvenile court judge as somewhat inconsistent and weak.

At the beginning of the hearing, McKeiver's lawyer said he had never met McKeiver before and was just interviewing him. The judge allowed five minutes for the interview. The lawyer then requested a jury trial, which the judge refused, and McKeiver was adjudicated and placed on probation. The case was appealed to the Pennsylvania Supreme Court, where it was joined to another juvenile case in which a jury trial had been requested.

Edward Terry, age fifteen and also from Philadelphia, hit a police officer with his fists and with a stick when the officer attempted to break up a fight Terry was watching. After denying a jury trial, the judge adjudicated Terry and committed him to an institution. These two cases were appealed to the U.S. Supreme Court, where they were consolidated with two North Carolina cases that also involved juveniles requesting jury trials (*In re Terry*, 265 A.2d 350 (1970)).

Barbara Burris and about forty-five other black children between the ages of eleven and fifteen had been arrested and charged with obstructing traffic as the result of a march protesting racial discrimination in the county schools. They refused to get off the paved portion of the highway when told to do so by police. In a separate incident arising out of the same protest, James Howard and some fifteen other juveniles created a disturbance in a principal's office. He was charged with being disorderly and defacing school property. The judge adjudicated all these juveniles and committed them to institutions. The judge then suspended the commitments and placed them on probation for terms ranging from twelve to twenty-four months (*In re Barbara Burrus* 169 S.E.2nd 879 (1969)).

The U.S. Supreme Court argued that juries would not enhance the accuracy of the adjudication process and could adversely affect the informal atmosphere of the non-adversarial juvenile court hearing process. The significance of *McKeiver* (1971) is that it is the only one of the five cases in which the U.S. Supreme Court did not rule that juveniles must receive all the same due process rights as adults in criminal court (*McKeiver v. Pennsylvania* 403 U.S. 528 (1971)).

Breed v. Jones, 421 U.S. 519 (1975)

On February 8, 1970, seventeen-year-old Gary Jones committed an armed robbery in Los Angeles with a loaded gun. He was arrested and placed in detention that same day. On March 1, 1970, Jones was adjudicated a delinquent on that charge, along with two other charges involving robberies with a loaded gun. The case was continued for two weeks so the probation officer could prepare a social history and recommend a disposition, and Jones was returned to detention.

On March 15, 1970, the court reconvened for the disposition hearing, but the judge announced instead that he would waive jurisdiction to the criminal court. Jones's lawyer expressed surprise and requested a continuance in order to prepare argument about the proposed waiver. The court continued the case for another week, then heard argument on the waiver issue and ordered Jones tried as an adult.

Jones' lawyer filed a writ of *habeas corpus* alleging Jones had already been tried in the juvenile court for this offense and could not be tried again in criminal court without violating the double jeopardy clause of the Fifth Amendment to the Constitution, which holds that no person shall be subject for the same offense to be twice put in jeopardy of life or limb.

This petition was denied because the court held that a juvenile adjudication was not a criminal trial, so that Jones had not been placed in jeopardy of life or limb at it. Jones was tried and convicted in adult criminal court and sentenced to prison. The case was appealed to the U.S. Supreme Court where the Justices ruled that adjudication is equivalent to a trial, because a juvenile is found to have violated a criminal statute. Jones's double jeopardy rights had therefore been violated, and the Court ruled that double jeopardy applies at the adjudication hearing as soon as any evidence is presented. A juvenile court waiver hearing must therefore take place before or in place of adjudication hearing (*Breed v. Jones* 421 U.S. 519, 95 S.Ct. 1779 [1975]).

These U.S. Supreme Court cases profoundly affected the legal process and procedures in juvenile courts throughout the United States. The overall purposes of the juvenile court remained the same, but court personnel were now required to inform the juvenile and their parents of due process rights. State legislation quickly followed to amend juvenile court procedures in accordance with these Supreme Court rulings.

EXTRALEGAL CONSIDERATIONS

In the 1960s, the President's Commission on Law Enforcement and Administration of Justice made the first comprehensive assessment of the U.S. juvenile justice system. The Commission focused in particular on the juvenile court, declaring it to be ineffective. The Task Force on Juvenile Delinquency (1967) concluded "that the great hopes originally held for the juvenile court have not been fulfilled. It has not succeeded significantly in rehabilitating delinquent youth, in reducing or even stemming the tide of juvenile criminality, or in bringing justice and compassion to the child offender" (p. 25). The Commission saw little promise in rehabilitation through treatment because it believed that the juvenile court unnecessarily stigmatized juveniles by labeling them delinquent, thus diminishing changes of rehabilitation.

On the issue of waivers, the Commission recommended:

> To be waived, a youth should be over a certain age (perhaps 16); the alleged offenses should be relatively grave (the equivalent of a felony, at least); the youth's prior offense record should be of a certain seriousness; the youth's treatment record discouraging. Waived youth would then be dealt with other than cursorily by the criminal court, and the juvenile court's action in waiving them would be based on an honest and open assessment of individual suitability. (Task Force on Juvenile Delinquency, 1967, p. 25)

Next, model waiver statues were developed. The 1968 Uniform Juvenile Court Act and the legislative Guide for Drafting Family and Juvenile Court Acts were the most used and influential model statutes. Both of these model acts incorporated certain restrictions on judicial waiver suggested by the Supreme Court in its *Kent* decision.

Just deserts reformers concentrated their efforts in the Juvenile Justice Standards Project initiated in 1971 by the Institute of Judicial Administration at New York University and later cosponsored by the American Bar Association. These came to be known as the IJA-ABA Standards. The IJA-AFA Standards urged increased judicial waiver but recommended that, to be eligible for waiver, the juvenile must be charged with an offense punishable in adult criminal court by a least twenty years imprisonment, which the waiver decision maker finds is "serious" (IJA-ABS, 1980, Secs. 1.1B, 2.2A, and 2.2C).

Third, in 1974, the Juvenile Justice Delinquency Prevention Act (JJDPA) established guidelines for set rules about delinquents in court. The 1974 Juvenile Justice Delinquency Act also established the Office of Juvenile Justice: now the Office of Juvenile Justice and Delinquency Prevention

(OJJDP). The Office of Juvenile Justice and Delinquency Prevention is located within the U.S. Department of Justice (DOJ) (Bilick, 2004; DePrato & Hammer, 2002).

In addition, the Twentieth Century Fund Task Force on Sentencing Policy toward young offenders also conducted its own review of available data and research on criminal and juvenile justice system policies governing the handling of serious and violent juvenile offenders, and took the position that waiver should be confined to serious, violent crime cases, involving juveniles past their mid-teens, where the minimum punishment necessary is substantially larger than that available to the juvenile court. They went on the say that all waiver decisions would be reviewed by an appellate tribunal. A sentencing structure for juveniles in criminal court was recommended, guided by the principle that the maximum sentencing options be significantly lower for violent young offenders than those for adults convicted of comparable crimes.

Positions taken by the Twentieth Century Fund soon were overshadowed by the just deserts philosophy originally provided by the American Friends Service Committee in its report on crime and punishment in American. It concluded that the individualized treatment model was theoretically faulty, systematically discriminatory in administration, and inconsistent with some of our most basic concepts of justice. Just deserts advocate initially directed their reforms at the criminal justice system having been provided impetus by the war on crime during the later 1960s and early 1970s. They quickly expanded their focus on the juvenile justice system.

Just deserts philosophy and practice grew in the 1980s and 1990 because of the rising crime, prison overcrowding, and disenchantment with the prospects of successful treatment programs. Considerable impetus was provided by reviews of program evaluations that found few rehabilitation programs to be effective. The most influential among these was the comprehensive review conducted by Martinson and his colleagues, published initially by Martinson. The general conclusion of these reviews was that nothing works (Martinson, 1974), thus, strong support was provided for the just deserts philosophy. The growth of juvenile violence in the 1980s and 1990s provided further justification for the waiver of juveniles to the adult criminal justice system.

In response to the increase in violent crime in the 1980 and 1990s, state legal reforms in juvenile justice, particularly those that deal with serious offenses, stressed punitiveness, accountability, and a concern for public safety, rejecting traditional concerns for diversion, and rehabilitation in favor for a get-tough approach to juvenile crime and punishment. This shift in emphasis from a focus on rehabilitating the individual to punishing the act is exemplified by the seventeen states that redefined the purpose clause of their juvenile courts to emphasize public safety, certainty of sanctions, and offender accountability (Torbet & Szymanski, 1998). Inherent in this change in focus is the belief that the juvenile justice system is too soft on delinquents who are thought to be potentially as much a threat to public safety as their adult criminal counterparts.

JUVENILE WAIVER

In response to the rise in violent crime by juveniles during the late 1980s and early 1990s, states around the country made changes to their waiver provisions (Griffin et al., 2011). These changes mainly involved the modification and increased use of juvenile waiver, changing sentencing structures, and modifying or removing traditional confidentiality provisions (Griffin, Torbet & Szymanski, 1998, 2001; Redding, 2008; Torbet & Szymanski, 1998). Between 1992 and 1997, forty-seven states and the District of Columbia changed their laws in at least one of these ways (National Research Council, 2000; Torbet & Szymanski, 1998).

Determining which juveniles belong in juvenile court has been an issue since its inception of the juvenile court (Tanenhaus, 2000). The court's founders recognized that not all juveniles should come within the juvenile court's jurisdiction, and so various mechanisms of waiving the juvenile to the adult criminal court were created (Griffin et al., 1998).

From the inception of the juvenile court, judges have had the discretion to waive jurisdiction to the adult criminal court. Juveniles waived to the adult criminal court via judicial waiver generally fit one of three case types: serious offense, extensive juvenile record, or juvenile near the age limit. In the serious offense case, the offense with which the juvenile is charged is so serious that the sanctions available to the juvenile court are felt to be insufficient. These cases usually involve violent crimes, most often murder. The second types of case, extensive juvenile record, involve juveniles with extensive histories of arrest and juvenile court sanctions who are deemed unable to benefit from juvenile court. In the third type of case, the juvenile is very close to the age limit of the juvenile court's jurisdiction. These cases are waived because the juvenile court would not have jurisdiction over the particular juvenile for a long enough period of time or because the juvenile is thought to be appropriate for adult criminal court (Zimring, 1998).

A judicial waiver occurs when a juvenile court relinquishes their right to prosecute the juvenile offender. Once this right to prosecute is relinquished, the juvenile can be certified, and tried as an adult (Burrow, 2008; Moore, 1996; Torbet & Szymanski, 1998).

In response to the perceived rise in violent juvenile crime, state legislatures began chipping away at the jurisdiction of the juvenile court, identifying more and more offenses better addressed in the adult court. Additionally, many legislatures lowered the age at which juveniles could be waived (Griffin, 2003;

Moore, 1996; Redding, 2008; Torbet & Szymanski, 1998). Due to these legislative changes, the number of juveniles convicted of felonies in criminal courts and incarcerated in adult correctional facilities has increased (Redding, 2008). In 1999, juveniles convicted in adult criminal court represented 1 percent of the new prison commitments (Snyder & Sickmund, 1999).

Prior to this movement, a waiver was handled on a case-by-case basis. The most important case guiding juvenile waiver is *Kent v. United States* (1966). In *Kent v. United States* (1966), the U.S. Supreme Court ruled that juveniles are entitled to due process procedures in waiver proceedings, that a hearing be held on waiver cases, that the juvenile have the right to representation by counsel at the hearing, that the juvenile's attorney be provided access to all information used by the judge in deciding on waiver, and that the juvenile court's waiver decision be supported by a statement of reasons. Another case related to juvenile waiver is *Breed v. Jones* (1975), which addressed the idea of a juvenile first being adjudicated a delinquent in juvenile court, and then being waived and tried as an adult; a violation of the double jeopardy clause of the Fifth Amendment.

Today, the majority of waivers are required, and most states have lowered the minimum age for waiver (Griffin et al., 2011). The minimum age at which a juvenile may be tried as an adult varies (Puzzanchera, 2001; Torbet & Szymanski, 1998). Some states have no minimum at all (Puzzanchera, 2001; Torbet & Szymanski, 1998), whereas others specify minimums as young as ten.

Waiver laws vary from state to state. Almost all states, however, use at least one of three waiver methods, and some states use a combination of two or three (Griffin et al., 2011; Puzzanchera, 2001; Sickmund, 1994; Torbet & Szymanski, 1998). The three methods in which cases can be waived include: judicial waiver, direct file, and statutory exclusion (Griffin et al., 2011; NCJFCJ, 2006; Puzzanchera, 2001; Sickmund, 1994; Torbet & Szymanski, 1998).

Judicial Waiver

The three types of judicial waiver are discretionary, presumptive, and mandatory (Griffin et al., 2011). In discretionary waiver, juvenile court judges have the discretion to waive the case to the adult criminal court. At the end of 2009, there were forty-five states that had the discretionary waiver mechanism (Griffin et al., 2011). In presumptive waiver, laws define which types of cases are presumed appropriate to waive from juvenile court to adult criminal court (Griffin et al., 2011). The decision is in the hands of the judge; however, waiver is presumed (Griffin et al., 2011). In presumptive waiver, the juvenile assumes the burden of proof to demonstrate why they should not be waived to the adult criminal court (Griffin et al., 2011). In addition, in some states, the presumption is applied against juveniles with certain kinds of histories, and with any offense committed with a firearm (Griffin et al., 2011). At the end of 2009, there were fifteen states that had the presumptive waiver mechanism (Griffin et al., 2011). Mandatory waiver applies to situations in which cases that meet certain criteria are waived to the adult criminal court. With mandatory waiver, a fitness hearing is conducted to determine whether the juvenile is amenable to treatment in the juvenile justice system (NCJFCJ, 2006; Torbet & Szymanski, 1998). At the end of 2009, there were fifteen states that had the mandatory waiver mechanism (Griffin et al., 2011)

The most popular method of waiver is discretionary, which exists in forty-seven states and the District of Columbia. Juvenile court judges weigh a variety of factors in determining whether to waive a juvenile. All states have incorporated the constitutionally required factors enumerated by the U.S. Supreme Court (Podkopacz & Feld, 1996). Griffin et al. (1998, 2011), NCJFCJ (2006), and Torbet and Szymanski (1998) list the constitutional requirements as the following:

- The seriousness of the offense
- The need to protect the community
- Whether the offense was committed in an aggressive violent, premeditated, or willful manner
- Whether the offense was against a person or property
- The merit of the complaint
- Whether the juvenile's associates will be tried in adult criminal court
- The juvenile's sophistication, maturity, record, and previous history, and
- The reasonable likelihood of rehabilitation

Direct File

The second method for waiving juveniles to the adult criminal court is called direct file (also known as prosecutorial waiver). As the general public, policy makers, and the courts determined that judicial hearings were not effective, they enacted alternative ways to waive juveniles from the juvenile court to the adult criminal court. For certain ages and offenses, direct file allows the prosecutor to choose the jurisdiction; juvenile or adult court. Unlike with judicial waiver, no hearing is held and there are no statutory factors to be considered. The decision to waive is left entirely to the prosecutor's discretion and it cannot be appealed. Many states use a combination of different waiver provisions, thus spreading the decision-making authority among the various agents of the court (Griffin et al., 1998, 2011; NCJFCJ, 2006; Torbet & Szymanski, 1998). Few states report data on cases waived by direct file (Griffin et al., 2011).

Statutory Exclusion

The third method a juvenile can be tried as an adult is through statutory exclusion; also known as mandatory waiver. In statutory exclusion, the state legislature establishes by law the age in which a juvenile offender is to be moved to the adult criminal court (Logan, 1998). Both the age and the crime (s) allegedly committed by the juvenile can be the subject of such law (Kole, 2001; Parent, Dunworth, McDonald & Rhodes, 1997).

In the 1980s and 1990s, waiver legislation has undergone major change with the get tough on crime movement. Many jurisdictions have passed statutory exclusion provisions that require the automatic waiver of certain juveniles into the adult criminal justice system. These statutory exclusion provisions apply to juveniles over a certain age charged with serious or violent felonies. The increasing waiver of juveniles into the adult criminal justice system is based on the desire to get tough with young offenders (Griffin et al., 1998; NCJFCJ, 2006; Torbet & Szymanski, 1998).

Whether legislative waiver is effective or not has been the subject of much debate (Jensen & Metsger, 1994; Risler, Sweatman & Nackerud, 1998; Singer & McDowell, 1998). Opponents suggest that legislative waivers cast a wide net, fail to take into consideration the juvenile's criminal background (Kole, 2001; McCarthy, 1994) and the general belief that juveniles are young and immature and thus less blame worthy than their adult counterparts (Scott & Steinberg, 2003). Like direct file, few states report data on cases waived by statutory exclusion (Griffin et al., 2011).

Exception to the Once Waived, Always Waived Practice/Policies

In order to restore balance and to allow for appropriate dispositions of some amenable, younger offenders, many states, roughly twenty-three, allow judges to reverse waive or waiver back to juvenile court cases that originated in the adult criminal court either as a result of excluded offense or prosecutorial direct file decisions. About half of the prosecutors use direct file, and excluded offense jurisdictions allow an adult criminal court judge either to return a juvenile to juvenile court for trial or sentencing, or to impose a juvenile or youthful offender sentence in lieu of an adult criminal sentence. In some states, offense exclusion or direct file laws that place a juvenile initially in adult criminal court create a presumption of unfitness and shift the burden of proof to the juvenile to demonstrate why they should be returned to juvenile court for trial or disposition. In other excluded offense jurisdictions, the prosecutor may make a reverse waiver decision. In most states, however, a criminal court judge makes the waiver back decision to sentence a youth as a juvenile (Feld, 2009; Griffin et al., 1998, 2011; NCJFCJ, 2006; Torbet & Szymanski, 1998).

An evaluation of reverse waiver decisions suggests that younger offenders, those who had fewer prior convictions and less previous exposure to correctional services, are returned to the juvenile court rather than remaining in the adult system (Griffin et al., 1998, 2011; Feld, 2009; NCJFCJ, 2006; Torbet & Szymanski, 1998). This is similar to juvenile court judicial waiver (Griffin et al., 1998, 2011; Feld, 2009; NCJFCJ, 2006; Torbet & Szymanski, 1998).

Once an Adult, Always an Adult

A special waiver provision has been created in thirty-four states for juveniles who, having once been prosecuted as adults, are subsequently prosecuted in the adult criminal court on any new offenses (Griffin et al., 2011). Most states with once and adult always an adult provision imply required criminal prosecution of all such subsequent offenses by either a blanket exclusion or an automatic waiver mechanism (Griffin et al., 1998, 2011). Nearly all once and adult always and adult provisions stipulate that the juvenile involved must have been convicted of the offense that triggered the adult prosecution (Griffin et al., 1998, 2011). In Iowa, California, and Oregon however, this is not always necessary. A subsequent charge that would ordinarily require a fitness hearing in juvenile court may be filed directly in criminal court if the juvenile involved was previously declared unfit for juvenile handling and waived to criminal court (Griffin et al., 2011); even if no conviction followed the original waiver. Likewise, in Delaware, the law does not require a conviction in the original case, provided a court had the opportunity to make a determination regarding the juvenile's amenability to rehabilitative processes of the juvenile court. Idaho requires adult prosecution of a juvenile who has already been convicted as an adult, even if the original conviction was for a lesser offense that would not have been excluded from juvenile court jurisdiction. Mississippi requires no conviction on the first adult prosecuted offense if the juvenile is subsequently accused of a felony.

REFERENCES

Adler, F., Mueller, G. O., & Laufer, W. (1995). *Criminology* (2nd ed.). New York: McGraw-Hill.

Aries, P. (1962). *Centuries of childhood: A social history of family life.* New York: Knopf.

Barlow, H. D. (1990). *Introduction to criminology* (5th ed.). Glenview, IL: Scott, Foresman, Little, and Brown.

Bartollas, C., & Miller, S. J. (2008). *Juvenile justice in America* (5th ed.). Upper Saddle River, NJ: Pearson Prentice Hall.

Bernard, T. J. (1992). *The cycle of juvenile justice.* New York: Oxford University.

Bilick, S. B. (2004). The utility of residential treatment programs in the prevention and management of juvenile delinquency. *Adolescent Psychiatry*, 267–278.

Binder, A., Gilbert, G., & Dickson, B. (1988). *Juvenile delinquency: Historical cultural and legal perspectives.* New York: Macmillan.

Black v. United States, 355 F.2d. 104, (1965).

Blackstone, W. (1803). *Commentaries on the laws of England* (12th ed.). London: Strahan.

Brace, C. L. (1872). *The dangerous classes of New York and twenty years of work among them.* New York: Wynkoop and Hallenbeck.

Breed v. Jones, 421 U.S. 519, 95 S.Ct. 1779 (1975).

Bremner, R. (1970). *Children and youth in America: A documentary history.* Cambridge, MA: Harvard University.

Burrow, J. (2008). Reverser and the effects of legal statutory and secondary legal factors on sentencing outcomes for juvenile offenders. *Crime and Delinquency, 54*(1), 34–64.

Bynum, J. E., & Thompson, W. E. (1992). *Juvenile delinquency* (2nd ed.). Boston, MA: Allyn and Bacon.

Cao, L. (2004). *Major criminological theories concepts and measurement.* Belmont, CA: Wadsworth/Thomson.

Champion, D. J., & Mays, G. L. (1991). *Transferring juveniles to criminal courts trends and implications for criminal justice.* Westport, CT: Praeger.

Cherry, R. (1890). *On the growth of criminal law in ancient communities.* New York: Macmillan.

Commonwealth v. M'Keagy, 1, Ashmead (PA) 248 (1831).

Cox, S. M., Allen, J. M., Hanser, R. D., & Conrad, J. J. (2008). *Juvenile justice a guide to theory, policy, and practice* (6th ed.). Thousand Oaks, CA: Sage.

Cullen, F. T., & Agnew, R. (2006). *Criminological theory past to present.* New York: Oxford University.

Davis, S. M. (1979). From rhetoric to reality: The juvenile court and the decline of the rehabilitative ideal. *Michigan Law Review, 77*(349), 912–916.

Dean, C. W., & Reppucci, N. D. (1974). Juvenile correctional institutions. In D. Glaser (Ed.), *Handbook of Criminology* (pp. 865–894). Chicago, IL: Rand McNally.

DePrato, K. K., & Hammer, J. H. (2002). Assessment and treatment of juvenile offenders. In D. H. Schetky & E. P. Benedck (Eds.), *Principles and practice of child and adolescent forensic psychiatry* (pp. 267–278). Washington, DC: American Psychiatric Press.

Durant, T., & Knottnerus, J. D. (1999). *Plantation society and race relations. The origins of inequality.* Westport, CT: Greenwood.

Elrod, P., & Ryder, R. S. (2005). *Juvenile justice a social, historical, and legal perspective* (2nd ed.). Sudbury, MA: Jones and Bartlett.

Elton, K., & Royball, M. M. (2003). Restoration, A component of justice. *Utah Law Review*, 42, 43–56.

Empey, L. T. (1978). *American delinquency: Its meaning and construction.* Homewood, IL: Dorsey.

Ex parte Becknell, 119 Cal. 496, 51 P. 692 (1897).

Feld, B. C. (2009). Juveniles in the adult system transfer back or "reverse waiver." *Crime and Justice, 3*, 263–284.

Fox, S. J. (1996, Winter). The early history of the court. *The Future of Children The Juvenile Court, 6*(3).

Finestone, H. (1976). *Victims of change: Juvenile delinquents in American society.* Westport, CT: Greenwood.

Garland, D. (1990). *Punishment and modern society a study in social theory*. Oxford: Oxford University Press.

Gold, S. D. (2007). *In re Gault: Do minors have the same rights as adults?*. New York: Marshall Cavendish Benchmark.

Gordon, L. (1988). *Family violence and social control.* New York: Viking.

Griffin, P., Addie, S., Adams, B., & Firestine, K. (2011). *Trying juveniles as adults: An analysis of state transfer laws and reporting* (Office of Juvenile Justice and Delinquency Prevention No. 232434). Washington, DC: U.S. Department of Justice.

Griffin, P., Torbet, P., & Szymanski, L. (1998). *Trying juveniles as adults in criminal court: An analysis of state transfer provisions* (Office of Juvenile Justice and Delinquency Prevention No. NCJ- 172836). Washington, DC: U. S. Department of Justice.

Hawes, J. (1971). *Children in urban society: Juvenile delinquency in 19th century America.* New York: Oxford University.

Hess, K. M. (2010). Juvenile justice (5th ed.). Belmont, CA: Wadsworth.

Hobbes, T. (1668). *Leviathan* (E. Curley, Ed.). Indianapolis, IN: Hackett.

Holl, J. (1971). *Juvenile reform in the progressive area.* Ithaca, NY: Cornell University.

Holt, M. I. (1992). *The orphan trains placing out in America.* University of Nebraska: Lincoln and London.

Houston, J., & Barton, S. M. (2005). *Juvenile justice theory, systems, and organization.* Upper Saddle River, NJ: Prentice Hall.

Howell, J. C. (1997). *Juvenile justice and youth violence.* Thousand Oaks, CA: Sage.

In re Barbara Burrus, 275 N.C. 517, 169 Sk. E. 2d. 879 (1969).

In re Michael C., 21 Cal. 3d 471, 579 (1978).

In re Terry, 438 Pa., 339, 265 A. 2d. 350 (1970).

In re Winship, 387 U.S. 358, 90 S.Ct. 1068 (1970).

Jensen, E., & Metsger, L. (1994). A test of the deterrent effects of legislative waiver on violent juvenile crime. *Crime and Delinquency, 40*, 96–104.

Jolowicz, H. F. (1957). *Roman foundations of modern law.* London: Oxford.

Juvenile Justice Standards Project (1971). *IJA-ABA-Standards.* Institute of Judicial Administration. Washington, DC: American Bar Association.

Kent v. United States, 383 U. S. 541 (1966).

Ketcham, O. W., & Paulsen, M. G. (1967). *Cases and materials relating to juvenile courts.* New York: The Foundation Press.

Kole, T. (2001). Juvenile offenders in the adult criminal justice system. *Harvard Journal on Legislation, 38*, 231–247.

Krisberg, B. (2004). *Juvenile justice: Redeeming our children.* Los Angeles, CA: Sage.
Krisberg, B., & Austin, J. F. (1993). *Reinventing juvenile justice.* Newburg Park, CA: Sage.
Lawrence, R., & Hemmens, C. (2008). *Juvenile justice a text/reader.* Los Angeles, CA: Sage.
Logan, W. (1998). Proportionality and punishment: Imposing life without parole on juveniles. *Wake Forest Law Review, 33*, 681–725.
Ludwig, F. J. (1955). *Youth and the law: Handbook on laws affecting youth.* Brooklyn, NY: Foundation Press.
Martin, G. (2005). *Juvenile justice process and systems.* Thousand Oaks, CA: Sage.
Mays, G. L., & Winfree, L. T. (2000). *Juvenile justice.* New York: McGraw-Hill.
McCarthy, F. (1994). The serious juvenile offender and juvenile court reform: The case for prosecutorial waiver of juvenile court jurisdiction. *St. Louis University Law Review, 345*, 629–671.
McKeiver v. Pennsylvania 403 U.S. 528, 91 S.Ct. (1976).
McLaughlin, M. M. (1975). Survivors and surrogates: Children and parents the ninth to the thirteenth centuries. In L. D. Mause (Ed.), *The history of childhood* (pp. 101–181). New York: Harper.
Mennel, R. (1973). *Thorns and thistles: Juvenile delinquents in the United States 1825–1940.* Hanover, NH: University Press of New England.
Miller, A., & Ohlin, L. (1985). *Delinquency and community.* Beverly Hills, CA: Sage.
Moore, M. H. (1996). The future of the juvenile court: A theoretical framework that fits. *The Future of Children The Juvenile Court, 64*(349), 140–146.
Moore, M. H., & Wakeling, S. (1997). *Juvenile justice: Shoring up the foundations.* Chicago, IL: The University of Chicago.
Mounteer, C. (1984). Beginners on the forum: Roman adolescence and youth, 200 B.C. to 100 A.D. *Journal of Psychohistory, 12*, 251–258.
Myers, D. L. (2005). *Boys among men trying and sentencing juveniles as adults.* Westport, CT: Praeger.
National Research Council Staff. (2000). *Juvenile crime, juvenile justice.* Washington, DC: National Academies Press (pp. 154–227).
NCJFCJ. (2006, January 1). Juvenile Justice Reform Initiatives in the states 1994–1996. In *Juvenile transfer to criminal court.* Washington, DC: U. S. Department of Justice.
Nyquist, O. (1960). *Juvenile justice: A comparative study with special reference to the Swedish Welfare Board and the California juvenile court system.* London: Macmillan.
Odem, M., & Schlossman, S. (1991). Guardians of virtue: The juvenile court and female delinquency in early 20th century Los Angeles. *Crime and Delinquency, 37*, 186–203.
Ozment, S. (1983). *When fathers ruled: Family life in reformation Europe.* Cambridge, MA: Harvard University.
Parent, D., Dunworth, T., McDonald, D., & Rhodes, W. (1997). *Key legislative issues in criminal justice: Transferring serious juvenile offenders to adult courts.* Washington, DC: National Institute of Justice.

People v. Turner, 55 Illinois 280 (1870).
Pickett, R. (1969). *House of refuge: Origins of juvenile reform in New York state, 1815–1857.* Syracuse, NY: Syracuse University.
Platt, A. M. (1969). *The child savers the invention of delinquency.* Chicago, IL: The University of Chicago.
Pleck, E. (1987). *Domestic Tyranny: The making of social policy against family violence from colonial times to the present.* New York: Oxford University.
Pleck, E. (1989). Criminal approaches to family violence, 1640–1980. In L. Ohlin & M. Tonry (Eds.), *Family violence* (pp. 19–58). Chicago, IL: University of Chicago.
Puzzanchera, C. M. (2001). *Delinquency cases waived to criminal court, 1989–1998* (Office of Juvenile Justice and Delinquency Prevention). Washington, DC: U. S. Department of Justice.
Podkopacz, M. R., & Feld, B. C. (1996). The end of the line: An empirical study of judicial waiver. *Criminal Law and Criminology, 86*(2), 449–492.
Redding, R. E. (2008). *Juvenile transfer laws: An effective deterrent to delinquency?* (Office of Juvenile Justice and Delinquency Prevention). Washington, DC: U. S. Department of Justice.
Regolia, R. M., & Hewitt, J. D. (2006). *Delinquency in society.* New York: McGraw-Hill.
Rendleman, D. R. (1974). Parens patriae: From chancery to the juvenile court. In F. L. Faust & P. J. Brantingham (Eds.), *Juvenile justice* (pp. 72–117). St. Paul, MN: West.
Risler, E., Sweatman, T., & Nackerud, L. (1998). Evaluating the Georgia legislative waivers effectiveness in deterring juvenile crime. *Research on Social Work Practices, 86,* 657–667.
Rothman, D. (1971). *The discovery of the asylum-social order and disorder in the new republic.* Boston: Little, Brown.
Rusche, G., & Kirchheimer, O. (1939). *Punishment and social structure.* Piscataway, NJ: Transaction.
Ryerson, E. (1978). *The best-laid plans America's juvenile court experiment.* New York: Hill and Wang.
Sanders, W. B. (1970). *Juvenile offenders for a thousand years.* Chapel Hill: University of North Carolina.
Schlossman, S. L. (1977). *Love and the American delinquent: The theory and practice of "progressive" juvenile justice.* Chicago, IL: University of Chicago.
Schwartz, I. M. (1989). *Justice for juveniles rethinking the best interests of the child.* Lexington, MA: Lexington University.
Scott, E., & Steinberg, L. (2003). Blaming youth. *Texas Law Review, 81*, 799–840.
Sellin, T. (1944). *Pioneering in penology: The Amsterdam houses of correction in the sixteenth and seventeenth centuries.* Philadelphia: University of Pennsylvania.
Shelden, R. G. (2001). *Controlling the dangerous classes: A critical introduction to the history of criminal justice.* Needham Heights, MA: Allyn and Bacon.
Sickmund, M. (1994). *How juveniles get to criminal court* (Office of Juvenile Justice and Delinquency Prevention). Washington, DC: U. S. Department of Justice.

Siegel, L. J. (2004). *Criminology theories, patterns, and typologies* (8th ed.). Belmont, CA: Wadsworth/Thomson.

Siegel, L. J., & Tracy, P. E. (2008). *Juvenile law a collection of leading U.S. Supreme Court cases.* Upper Saddle River, NJ: Pearson Prentice Hall.

Siegel, L. J., & Welsh, B. C. (2009). *Juvenile delinquency theory practice and law.* Belmont, CA: Wadsworth.

Singer, S. I., & McDowall, D. (1988). Criminalizing delinquency: The deterrent effects of the New York juvenile offender law. *Law and Society Review, 22*(349), 521–535.

Snyder, H. N., & Sickmund, M. (1999). *Juvenile offenders and victims: 1999 national report.* Washington, DC: U. S. Department of Justice.

Stampp, K. M. (1956). *The peculiar institutions: Slavery in the antebellum south.* New York: Vintage Books.

State v. Ray, 63 N.H. 406 (1886).

Tanenhaus, D. S. (2000). The evolution of transfer out of the juvenile court. In J. Fagan & F. E. Zimring (Eds.), *The changing borders of juvenile justice: Transfer of adolescents to the criminal court* (pp. 13–43). Chicago, IL: The University of Chicago.

Taylor, R. W., Fritsch, E. J., & Caeti, T. J. (2007). *Juvenile justice policies programs, and practices* (2nd ed.). New York: McGraw-Hill.

Thomas, C. W., & Bilchik, S. (1985). Prosecuting juveniles in criminal courts: A legal and empirical analysis. *The Journal of Criminal Law and Criminology, 76*(2), 439–479.

Thornton, W. E., & Voigt, L. (1992). *Delinquency and justice.* New York: McGraw-Hill.

The Holy Bible. New International Version.

Torbet, P., & Szymanski, L. (1998). *State legislative responses to violent juvenile crime: 1996–1997 update* (Office of Juvenile Justice and Delinquency Prevention). Washington, DC: U. S. Department of Justice.

Vold, G. B., Bernard, T. J., & Snipes, J. B. (1998). *Theoretical criminology* (4th ed.). New York: Oxford University.

Watson, A. (1970). *The laws of ancient Romans.* Dallas, TX: Southern Methodist University.

Wines, E. C. (1970). *The state of prisons and childsaving institutions in the civilized world.* Carbondale, IL: Southern Illinois University.

Yetman, N. (1970). *Life under the "peculiar institution.".* San Antonio: Holt, Rienhart, and Winston.

Yetman, N. (2000). *Voices from slavery: 100 authentic slave narratives.* New York: Dover.

Zimring, F. E. (1998). *American youth violence.* New York: Oxford University.

Chapter 2

Juvenile Transfer

Law and Policy

Lisa S. Nored

The practice of transferring juvenile offenders to the adult court system garners mixed results when considering the underlying philosophy of the juvenile court system, public opinion regarding the treatment of youthful offenders, and long-term implications for offender outcomes. Transfer laws have been in existence for many years and gained increased popularity with calls for "get-tough" measures to combat the perceived increases in crime rates by juveniles. Frustrated with the lack of meaningful options for juvenile offenders and responding to perceived waves of violent crimes perpetrated by "super predators," the pendulum began to shift in the mid-1980s. The court of public opinion as well as savvy politicians who monitored its pulse responded with harsher penalties for juvenile offenders.

Laws regarding the practice of transfer and waiver were ripe for use as weapons in the "war on crime." The most common strategies utilized by states seeking to target youth crime with stronger transfer provisions were the reduction in age at which a juvenile was eligible to be transferred to adult court; expansion of the offenses for which a juvenile could be transferred to adult court; and increased use or adoption of laws allowing for direct file of cases involving juvenile offenders in adult court. By strengthening these laws, policymakers and state legislatures were able to convey a strong message to delinquent youth by effectively removing protections offered within the juvenile justice system. However, the removal of those protections brought consequences, some intended and others not. The adult court system would now be asked to assume custody, care, and control of a population of youthful offenders, which it was ill-equipped to manage.

JUVENILE TRANSFER DEFINED

Often used synonymously with the term "waiver," transfer refers to the shift of jurisdiction from the juvenile court to the adult court while waiver more specifically refers to a voluntary relinquishment by the juvenile court of its original statutory jurisdiction. Waiver and transfer laws are both procedural mechanisms utilized to shift jurisdiction to the adult court over young offenders who are no longer deemed amenable to the services and treatment alternatives within the juvenile court. Whether waived or transferred, once within the jurisdiction of the adult court, juveniles are considered adults for purposes of legal processes, including sentencing and correctional alternatives. The adult court now possesses jurisdictional control over the case and the offender.

LEGAL TREATMENT OF TRANSFER

Transfer proceedings were addressed by the U.S. Supreme Court in two important cases: *Kent v. United States* (1966) and *Breed v. Jones* (1975). *Kent* and *Breed* were among several successive cases decided by the Court during what has since become known as the "due process revolution." During this time, the Court was active with its willingness to review cases involving greater protection of civil liberties, heightened attention to the rights of criminal defendants, and the expansion of due process protections to various stages of the legal process.

In *Kent v. United States* (1966), the U.S. Supreme Court granted the petition for writ of certiorari in a case involving a sixteen-year-old accused of housebreaking, robbery and rape. Kent was waived to adult court pursuant to a statute, which allowed for transfer of juveniles "after a full investigation." Procedural protections were not specifically outlined in the statute.

Prior to the waiver determination, counsel for Kent filed a motion on the issue of waiver specifically raising concerns about Kent's mental condition. Despite the pending motion and request by counsel for access to the social service file and other juvenile court records, including a probation report, no hearing was held, and no reasons were given by the juvenile court to support the decision to waive Kent to adult court. Moreover, counsel was not provided with access to the file which contained juvenile court records and staff recommendations.

The procedural facts and circumstances in *Kent*, and later in *In re Gault* (1967), illustrated the need for basic due process protections in juvenile courts. Acknowledging the need to address procedures in juvenile courts despite the "civil" classification of juvenile proceedings, the Court opined:

"there is evidence, in fact, that there may be grounds for concern that the child receives the worst of both worlds: that he gets neither the protections accorded to adults nor the solicitous care and regenerative treatment postulated for children."

In *Kent*, the Court specifically held that waiver is a "critically important stage," given the loss sustained by juveniles removed from the jurisdiction of the juvenile court and the protections which exist within that court system. As such, certain standards must accompany the waiver process. In *Kent*, the Court held that juveniles are entitled to counsel; a waiver hearing; access to juvenile court records and evidence, which the court will consider; and, in order to allow meaningful review of waiver decisions, a statement of reasons, although basic, must accompany the waiver decision. The Court was careful to balance the nature and extent of the procedural protections outlined in *Kent* against the customary flexibility and informality possessed by juvenile courts.

Following *Kent*, *In re Gault* (1967) was handed down by the Court resulting in a transformation of practice and procedure in American juvenile courts. *Gault* required basic due process protections in juvenile courts to ensure that children did not receive "the worst of both worlds" as originally acknowledged in *Kent*.

Years later, in *Breed v. Jones* (1975), the Court again addressed the issue of juvenile waiver and transfer. In *Breed*, the Supreme Court granted the petition for writ of certiorari on the narrow issue of whether the protection against double jeopardy as contained in the Fifth and Fourteenth Amendments rendered unconstitutional the prosecution in adult court of a juvenile already subjected to an adjudicatory hearing in juvenile court. Parties in the case agreed that the double jeopardy clause applied to juvenile court proceedings; that the proceedings in juvenile court and adult court relate to the same offense for purposes of double jeopardy; and that the juvenile was placed in jeopardy by the prosecution in adult court. However, the parties disagreed on whether the juvenile was "twice put in jeopardy" as a result of the adjudicatory hearing in juvenile court. The essence of the inquiry in *Breed* was whether the adjudicatory hearing in juvenile court results in "jeopardy" as contemplated by the protections set forth in the Fifth and Fourteenth Amendments.

For purposes of double jeopardy interpretation and jurisprudence, "jeopardy denotes risk." *Breed* at 528. In *Breed*, the Court, relying on precedent in *Price* (1970) and *Serfass* (1975), emphasized that the double jeopardy protections are designed to protect against the risk of subsequent legal prosecution and conviction. As such, the analysis required assessment and comparison of the risk and burdens encountered during an adjudicatory hearing in juvenile court and prosecution in adult court. In *Breed*, the Court held as follows:

> As we have observed, the risk to which the term jeopardy refers is that traditionally associated with "actions intended to authorize criminal punishment to vindicate public justice" because of its purpose and potential consequences, and the nature and resources of the State, such a proceeding imposes heavy pressures and burdens —psychological, physical, and financial—on a person charged. The purpose of the Double Jeopardy Clause is to require that he be subject to the experience only once "for the same offense." (internal citations omitted)

Breed v. Jones, 421 U.S. 519, 530 (1975). Given the similarity of risk, the Court held that a juvenile who was subjected to an adjudicatory hearing in juvenile court and subsequently subjected to prosecution in adult court was placed in legal jeopardy more than once as contemplated by the double jeopardy clause.

The trilogy of *Kent*, *Gault*, and *Breed* brought important changes to the use of transfer procedures in juvenile courts. While formality and structure were originally avoided in the design of the juvenile court in favor of vast discretion vested in personnel operating in a confidential setting to carry out *parens patriae* functions, time and experience eventually revealed that the lack of standards often produced contradictory and unjust results for juveniles. Through the Fifth and Fourteenth Amendments, the end of blind adherence to the "civil" label assigned to juvenile proceedings and enhanced scrutiny of procedures that provided for or allowed the unbridled discretion of juvenile court actors and judges, this era of jurisprudence imposed necessary structure and standards to guide discretion, fulfill due process ideals, and promote fairness thus leading us closer to the original efforts to help, not harm children.

Since the decisions in *Kent*, *Gault*, and *Breed*, the U.S. Supreme Court has not specifically revisited the issue of juvenile transfer. However, beginning in 2005, the Court has struck down more extreme and severe sentencing options for juvenile offenders who are prosecuted in adult court. Each of these cases embraced the view that youthful offenders have reduced culpability and should be treated differently due to their immaturity and embracing an offender-based, as opposed to offense-based approach, which fully recognizes age as a mitigating factor despite commission of serious crimes.

In *Roper v. Simmons* (2005), the Court declared use of the death penalty for individuals under the age of eighteen at the time of the crime as a violation of the Eighth Amendment and the protection from cruel and unusual punishment. Relying on indicators such as existing laws, the willingness of juries to impose the death penalty, as well as the evolution of science regarding brain development, the Court removed the death penalty as a sentencing option for offenders under the age of eighteen. *Roper* has earned a place among landmark decisions by removing the ultimate penalty as a sentencing option for juvenile offenders prosecuted in adult court and bringing the United States into alignment with international treatment of juvenile offenders.

With the death penalty no longer available, legal challenges in cases involving young offenders focused on life without parole and mandatory sentencing. In *Graham v. Florida* (2010), the Court held that the imposition of life without parole sentences for juvenile offenders in non-homicide cases also violate the Eighth Amendment. As in *Roper*, the *Graham* Court was particularly attentive to the unique status of youthful offenders, neuroscientific developments, and foreclosed prospects for rehabilitation when juveniles have no meaningful opportunity for release.

In *Miller v. Alabama* (2012), the Court concluded that mandatory sentencing schemes requiring life imprisonment without parole for individuals who were under the age of eighteen at the time of the crime violated the Eighth Amendment. The Court did not categorically hold that life imprisonment without parole could not be imposed as a sentence upon a juvenile offender, rather the Court held that the mandatory nature of such sentences without a mechanism for individualized sentencing for those under the age of eighteen violated the Constitution.

Many scholars and advocates view the *Roper*, *Graham*, and *Miller* trilogy as an opportunity for additional juvenile justice reforms. With the current judicial acknowledgment of developmental limitations and reduced culpability of young offenders, an examination of the prevailing literature reveals a growing call for continued examination of our legal treatment of juvenile offenders in an effort to reduce or reverse the impact of get-tough policies (Scott 2013; Drinan 2016). What follows remains to be seen; however, the Court appears poised to move toward greater scrutiny, less discretion when juvenile offenders are in the adult criminal justice system, and more categorical exclusion of harsh sentencing options for juveniles.

REFERENCES

Breed v. Jones, 421 U.S. 519 (1975).

Drinan, Cara H., *The Miller Revolution*, 101 Iowa L. Rev. 1787 (2016).

Graham v. Florida, 560 U.S. 48 (2010).

In re Gault, 387 U.S. 1 (1967).

Kent v. United States, 383 U.S. 541 (1966).

Miller v. Alabama, 567 U.S. 460 (2012).

Price v. Georgia, 398 U.S. 323 (1970).

Roper v. Simmons, 543 U.S. 551 (2005).

Serfass v. United States, 420 U.S. 377 (1975).

Scott, Elizabeth S., *Miller v. Alabama* and (the Past) and Future of Juvenile Crime Regulation, 31 Law & Inequality, 535 (2013).

Chapter 3

Exceptions to the Once Waived, Always Waived Practice/Policy

Sheri Jenkins Keenan

"Waiver" is a generic term that encompasses multiple transfer mechanisms. The research literature mainly focuses on three types of wavier; judicial; prosecutorial, also known as direct file; and legislative, also known as statutory exclusion. Judicial waiver laws allow juvenile court judges, after a formal hearing based on articulated standards, to waive jurisdiction to the adult criminal court. There are three types of judicial waiver: discretionary, presumptive, and mandatory. Forty-five states have one or more of the aforementioned kinds of judicial waiver. Prosecutorial or direct file laws define a class of cases that may be brought in either juvenile or criminal court by the prosecutor. No hearing is held to determine which court is appropriate and no formal standard deciding between them. There are fifteen states that have prosecutorial or direct file laws. Legislative waiver or statutory exclusion laws grant criminal courts exclusive jurisdiction over certain classes of cases regardless of an offender's age. If a case falls under the statutory exclusion law, it must be filed originally in adult criminal court. All states have at least one of the aforementioned kinds of transfer law.

Reverse waiver is the little studied fourth type of waiver. A reverse waiver is when a juvenile being tried in the adult criminal court request to be transferred into the juvenile justice system. The twenty-four states that have reverse waiver laws include Arizona, Arkansas, California, Colorado, Connecticut, Delaware, Georgia, Iowa, Kentucky, Maryland, Mississippi, Montana, Nebraska, Nevada, New York, Oklahoma, Oregon, Pennsylvania, South Dakota, Tennessee, Vermont, Virginia, Wisconsin, and Wyoming.

In order to restore balance and to allow for appropriate dispositions of some amenable, younger offenders, many states allow judges to reverse waive or waiver back to juvenile court cases that originated in the adult criminal court either as a result of excluded offense or prosecutorial direct file decisions. For example, Indiana allows a child as young as ten to be waived for murder. Kansas allows a child as young as ten to be waived for any criminal offense. Vermont allows a child as young as ten to be waived for murder, certain person offenses, and certain property offenses. Finally, there are fourteen states that have no age restriction specified. These states include Alaska, Delaware, Idaho, Maine, Maryland, Oklahoma, Oregon, Rhode Island, South Carolina, South Dakota, Tennessee, Washington, and West Virginia.

About half of the states that utilize prosecutorial waiver/direct file and excluded offense jurisdictions allow an adult criminal court judge either to return a juvenile-to-juvenile court for trial or sentencing, or to impose a juvenile or youthful offender sentence in lieu of an adult criminal sentence. In some states, offense exclusion or direct file laws that place a juvenile initially in adult criminal court create a presumption of unfitness and shift the burden of proof to the juvenile to demonstrate why they should be returned to juvenile court for trial or disposition. In other excluded offense jurisdictions, the prosecutor may make a reverse waiver decision. In most states, however, a criminal court judge makes the waiver back decision to sentence a youth as a juvenile.

An evaluation of reverse waiver decisions suggests that younger offenders those who had fewer prior convictions and less previous exposure to correctional services are returned to the juvenile court rather than remaining in the adult system.

Finally, most states also have laws requiring minors who have been previously charged as adults to be prosecuted in adult court for a successive offense, regardless of the nature of the offense. This is referred to as "Once an Adult, Always an Adult" Transfer (Griffin et al., 2011). Most states with once an adult always an adult provision imply required criminal prosecution of all such subsequent offenses by either a blanket exclusion or an automatic waiver mechanism (Griffin et al., 1998, 2011). Nearly all once an adult, always and adult provisions stipulate that the juvenile involved must have been convicted of the offense that triggered the adult prosecution (Griffin et al., 1998, 2011). In Iowa, California, and Oregon however, this is not always necessary. A subsequent charge that would ordinarily require a fitness hearing in juvenile court may be filed directly in criminal court if the juvenile involved was previously declared unfit for juvenile handling and waived to criminal court (Griffin et al., 2011); even if no conviction followed the original waiver. Likewise, in Delaware, the law does not require a conviction in the original case, provided a court had the opportunity to decide regarding the juvenile's amenability to rehabilitative processes of the juvenile court. Idaho requires adult prosecution of a juvenile who has already been convicted as an adult, even if the original conviction was for a lesser offense that would not have been excluded from juvenile court jurisdiction. Mississippi requires no conviction on the first adult prosecuted offense if the juvenile is subsequently accused of a felony.

REFERENCES

Adams, B., & Addie, S. (2010). *Delinquency cases waived to criminal court, 2007.* Washington, DC: U.S. Department of Justice, Office of Justice Programs, Office of Juvenile Justice and Delinquency Prevention.

Bishop, D. (2000). Juvenile offenders in the adult criminal justice system. In M. Tonry (Ed.), *Crime and justice: A review of research* (pp. 81–167). Chicago, IL: University of Chicago Press.

Feld, B. C. (2004). Editorial introduction: Juvenile transfer. *Criminology and Public Policy, 345*, 599–604.

Feld, B. C. (2009). Juveniles in the adult system transfer back or "reverse waiver." *Crime and Justice, 3*, 22–37.

Griffin, P., Torbet, P., Saddie, D., Adams, B., & Firestine, K. (2011). *Trying juveniles as adults in criminal court: An analysis of state transfer provisions.* Washington, DC: U.S. Department of Justice, Office of Justice Programs, Office of Juvenile Justice and Delinquency Prevention.

Chapter 4

Once an Adult, Always an Adult

Riane M. Bolin

The previous chapters discussed a number of mechanisms by which a juvenile may be transferred or waived to criminal court, with one such mechanism being statutory exclusion. Recall that statutory exclusion laws "grant criminal courts exclusive jurisdiction over cases involving juvenile age offenders" (Griffin et al., 2011, p. 2). Thus, if a juvenile commits an offense that falls within a statutory exclusion category, the case must be prosecuted in criminal court. Once an adult, always an adult (also referred to as once waived/always waived) laws represent a specific form of statutory exclusion (Griffin et al., 2011). Though there is variability across states, generally speaking, once an adult, always an adult law requires that juveniles who were previously prosecuted as adults be excluded from juvenile court jurisdiction and be automatically transferred to adult court for any subsequent offenses, usually regardless of the severity of said offenses (Griffin et al., 1998; Mays & Ruddell, 2012). In other words, juveniles who have been tried or convicted as adults become permanently terminated from juvenile court jurisdiction (Griffin et al., 1998). Currently, thirty-four states along with the District of Columbia have once an adult, always an adult law (see figure 4.1) (National Juvenile Defender Center, 2018). This chapter will provide an overview of the development of once an adult law, how these laws vary by state, and some of the potential benefits and drawback of such laws.

THE DEVELOPMENT OF ONCE AN ADULT, ALWAYS AN ADULT LAWS

Once an adult, always an adult law was a result of public fear that a juvenile crime wave was imminent (Merlo et al., 1999). This fear that occurred during

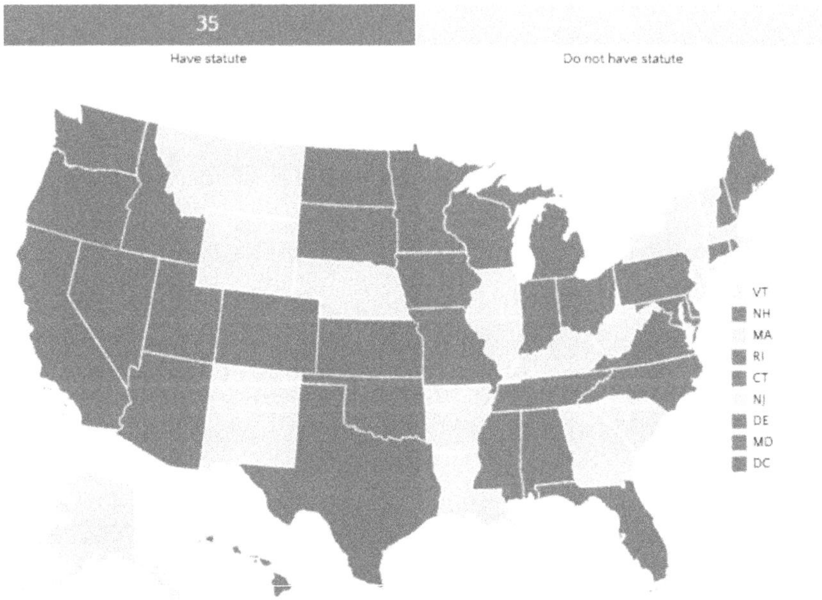

Figure 4.1 States with Current Once an Adult, Always an Adult Laws. *Source*: JJGPS: Juvenile Justice Geography, Police, Practice, & Statistics.

the 1980s and 1990s was fueled by an increase in violent juvenile crime, the media sensationalizing crimes committed by juveniles, and predictions of an invasion of juvenile "super-predators" (Bennett et al., 1996; Butts & Travis 2002; Dilulio, 1995). In response to the nation's concern regarding juvenile crime along with concern that the juvenile justice system was not equipped to handle serious juvenile offenders, a number of new laws aimed at increasing the severity of punishments for juveniles were enacted (Clarke, 2005).

Between 1992 and 1997, laws focusing on the handling of juveniles who committed violent crimes or who were repeat offenders were passed in virtually all states (Zimring, 1998). One area of focus for state legislatures was making it easier to transfer juveniles to adult court jurisdiction and subsequently keep them there if future offenses were committed (Merlo et al., 1999; Torbet & Szymanski, 1998). Thus, once an adult, always an adult law was enacted. In 1997, thirty states and the District of Columbia had once an adult, always an adult laws (Alabama, Arizona, California, Delaware, Florida, Hawaii, Idaho, Indiana, Iowa, Kansas, Maine, Michigan, Minnesota, Mississippi, Missouri, Nevada, New Hampshire, North Dakota, Ohio, Oklahoma, Oregon, Pennsylvania, Rhode Island, South Dakota, Tennessee, Texas, Utah, Virginia, Washington, and Wisconsin), with Arizona, Indiana, Michigan, and Oklahoma having enacted their laws during the 1996–1997 period (Griffin et al., 1998). By 1999, three more states, Illinois, Maryland, and North Carolina, had added such provisions (Griffin et al., 2011; Szymanski, 2002). The last states to add once an adult, always an adult law were Colorado and Connecticut, who both enacted them in 2015 (Juvenile Justice Geography, Policy, Practice & Statistics, n.d.). Table 4.1 includes a list of all states with current once an adult, always an adult provision along with the corresponding statute where the provision may be found.

Table 4.1 Once an Adult, Always an Adult Provisions by State

State	*Statute*
Alabama	Ala. Code § 12–15–204(b)
Arizona	Ariz. Rev. Stat. Ann. § 13–50
California	Cal. Welf. & Inst. Code § 707.01(a)(5)
Colorado	Colo. Rev. Stat. Ann. § 19–2–517(1)(a)
Connecticut	Conn. Gen. Stat. Ann. § 46b–127(a)(1).
Delaware	Code Ann. tit. 10, § 1010(c)(3).
District of Columbia	D.C. Code § 16–2307(h).
Florida	Fla. Stat. Ann. § 985.557(3)(a); Fla. Stat. Ann. § 985.556(5)(a).
Hawaii	Haw. Rev. Stat. Ann. § 571–22(e)
Idaho	Idaho Code Ann. 20–509(3).
Indiana	Ind. Code Ann. § 31–30–3–6.
Iowa	Iowa Code Sec. 232.45A
Kansas	Kan. Stat. Ann. § 38–2302(s)(3).
Maine	Me. Rev. Stat. Ann. tit. 15 § 3101(4)(G).
Maryland	Md. Code Ann., Cts. & Jud. Proc. § 3–8A–03(d)(5)
Michigan	Mich. Comp. Laws Ann. § 712A.4(5).
Minnesota	Minn. Stat. Ann. § 260B.125(5).
Mississippi	Miss. Code Ann. § 43–21–157(8).
Missouri	Mo. Ann. Stat. § 211.071(9)–(10).
Nevada	Nev. Rev. Stat. Ann. § 62B.390(4)
New Hampshire	N.H. Rev. Stat. Ann. § 169–B:27.
North Carolina	N.C. Gen. Stat. Ann. § 7B–1604(b).
North Dakota	N.D. Cent. Code Ann. § 27–20–34(4).
Ohio	Ohio Rev. Code Ann. § 2152.02(C)(5)
Oklahoma	Okla. Stat. Ann. tit. 10A § 2–5–204(G)(1)–(2)
Oregon	Or. Rev. Stat. Ann. § 419C.364.
Pennsylvania	42 Pa. Stat. and Cons. Stat. Ann. § 6322(a).
Rhode Island	R.I. Gen. Laws Ann. § 14–1–7.1(c).
South Dakota	S.D. Codified Laws 26–11–4.
Tennessee	Tenn. Code Ann. § 37–1–134(c).
Texas	Tex Fam. Code Ann. § 54.02(m)(1)–(2)
Utah	Utah Code Ann. 78A–6–701(3)(a)
Virginia	Va. Code Ann. § 16.1–271.
Washington	Wash. Rev. Code Ann. §13.40.020(15)
Wisconsin	Wis. Stat. Ann. § 938.183(1)(b), (c).

Source: Data compiled by author.

As juvenile crime rates decreased and the "get tough" sentiment began to wane, the enactment of once an adult, always an adult provision largely came to a halt (Griffin, 2008). In fact, no new laws were passed between the period of 2000 and 2014 (JJGPPS, n.d.) and with the exception of Colorado and Connecticut in 2015, no states have since enacted such legislation. In fact, some states have even amended their laws to narrow the scope. For example, in 2007, in a unanimous vote, the Virginia legislature passed a bill to amend their once an adult, always an adult law (H.B. 3007, 2007 Gen. Assem., Reg. Sess. (Va. 2007)). Prior to the amendment, a juvenile did not have to be convicted of a crime in adult court in order for the provision to be applied (Neelum, 2011). Rather, the juvenile simply had to have been transferred to the adult court on a charge. Thus, a juvenile who was prosecuted in adult court, but was acquitted would remain in the adult court for any future charges. The amended law requires that a conviction in adult court is necessary if the juvenile is to be tried in adult court for subsequent offenses. If the juvenile is acquitted of charges in adult court, then he or she regains his or her juvenile status and does not face automatic transfer to adult court if charged for subsequent offenses. A similar amendment was passed by the Washington legislature in 2009 (S.S.B. No. 5746, 60th Leg., Reg., Sess. (Wash. 2009)), mandating that only youth convicted in adult court can be automatically treated as adults for any future offenses (Neelum, 2011).

While some states limited the scope by necessitating there be a conviction in adult court, others chose to focus on the type of offense committed. For example, in 2008, Indiana revised their law to focus only on convictions of felony offenses (H.E. 1122, 115th Gen. Assem., 2d Reg. Sess. (Ind. 2008)). The original law allowed for the automatic waiver of a child to adult court if that child was previously convicted in adult court of a felony *or* non-traffic misdemeanor (Neelum, 2011). The amended law, however, limits automatic wavier to adult court to only juveniles who have been previously convicted of a felony in adult court. More recently, North Carolina revised their once an adult, always an adult provision as part of their Raise the Age Modification bill (Juvenile Jurisdiction Advisory Committee, 2019). Previously, a juvenile who had a prior conviction in adult court for a misdemeanor or infraction violation of motor vehicle laws was excluded from juvenile court jurisdiction. However, the amendment removes the automatic waiver of those youth convicted of motor vehicle violations, with the exception of driving while impaired, thus narrowing the scope of to whom the law applies.

Though some states such as Virginia, Washington, Indiana, and North Carolina have been successful in amending their laws, only one state has successfully eliminated their once an adult, always an adult law. In 2016, as part of a package of new laws aimed at limiting the number of juveniles in the adult prison system, Illinois became the first state to completely eliminate their once an adult, always an adult provision, thereby no longer automatically transferring minors previously convicted as adults to adult court for subsequent offenses (Garcia, 2015; JJGPPS, n.d.). One other state, Nevada, has had discussions about eliminating the law, but so far, any proposal for elimination has failed to garner support (Nevada Legislature Legislative Committee on Child Welfare and Juvenile Justice's Task Force to Study Juvenile Justice Issues, 2014).

VARIATION IN ONCE AN ADULT, ALWAYS AN ADULT LAWS

The eligibility requirements for once an adult, always an adult law is relatively consistent across states. However, some variation does exist (Griffin, 2008). One way in which the laws vary is according to whether or not they require that the juvenile involved be convicted of the offense that initiated the original adult prosecution (Griffin et al., 1998). The majority of states stipulate that a conviction is required in order for juvenile court jurisdiction to be terminated for future offenses. However, in a few states, a conviction is not always necessary. California law states that even if a juvenile is not convicted of an offense in adult court, but there has been a prior determination that the juvenile was unfit to be handled under juvenile court law based solely upon the minor's previous delinquent history or lack of success of previous attempts by the juvenile court to rehabilitate the minor, then should the minor be charged with a subsequent offense, and a petition may be filed directly in criminal court if certain criteria are met (Cal. Welf. & Inst. Code § 707.01(a)(5).). Similarly, Delaware's law does not require that a juvenile be convicted of an offense in adult court, but rather that the juvenile either previously has been declared nonamenable to the rehabilitative processes of the juvenile court or denied a reverse waiver (i.e., transferring the juvenile from adult court back to juvenile court) (Code Ann. tit. 10, § 1010(c)(3)).

Another distinction involves the type of offenses that trigger the once an adult, always an adult provision (Griffin et al., 1998). Most states simply require that a minor be convicted of a crime in adult court, without specifying whether the crime need be a misdemeanor or felony (JJGPPS, n.d.). However, in some states, the provision is tailored to only those who are convicted of certain offenses or receive certain types of sentences. Iowa, for example, limits the provision to only those youth who have been convicted in criminal court of a felony or aggravated misdemeanor (Iowa Code Sec. 232.45A). In Arizona, Connecticut, Maryland, and Minnesota, the juvenile must be convicted of a felony offense in order for the provision to apply (Ariz. Rev. Stat. Ann. § 13–50; Conn. Gen. Stat. Ann. § 46b–127(a)(1);

Md. Code Ann., Cts. & Jud. Proc. § 3-8A-03(d)(5); Minn. Stat. Ann. § 260B.125(5)).

Ohio is unique in that it does focus not only on the type of offense for which the juvenile was convicted but also on the type of sentence the juvenile receives. Specifically, the once an adult, always an adult provision in Ohio can be applied to youth who have either been previously convicted of a felony in which an adult sentence was imposed or who have been previously adjudicated as a youthful offender and the adult portion of their blended sentence was invoked (Ohio Rev. Code Ann. § 2152.02(C)(5)).

Variation also exists in regard to the type of offense that can trigger the once an adult, always an adult provision, following a juvenile's initial conviction as an adult (Griffin et al., 1998). Most states require that any subsequent offense, regardless of the severity, be automatically tried in criminal court via either a blanket exclusion or an automatic waiver (Griffin, 2008). However, some states restrict their once an adult, always an adult laws to only certain types of subsequent offenses. For example, five states—Indiana, Maryland, Michigan, Minnesota, and Texas—restrict the coverage of their laws to only juveniles who after a conviction in adult court are thereafter charged with a felony offense (Ind. Code Ann. § 31-30-3-6; Md. Code Ann., Cts. & Jud. Proc. § 3-8A-03(d)(5); Mich. Comp. Laws Ann. § 712A.4(5); Minn. Stat. Ann. § 260B.125(5); Tex Fam. Code Ann. § 54.02(m)(1)-(2)). Iowa restricts the coverage to only subsequent felonies or aggravated misdemeanors. Additionally, California stipulates that the subsequent offense must be a violation for which waiver is allowed (Cal. Welf. & Inst. Code § 707.01(a)(5)).

While the majority of states do not have specifications on how old a juvenile must be in order for the once an adult, always an adult provision to be applied, two states do limit the laws to juveniles of a certain age. In both California and Oregon, juveniles must be at least sixteen years old in order for the once an adult, always an adult provision to apply (Cal. Welf. & Inst. Code § 707.01(a)(5); Or. Rev. Stat. Ann. § 419C.364). Oregon is also unique in that their once an adult, always an adult provision is not mandatory. According to Oregon statute, for juveniles previously waived to adult criminal court, the juvenile court has the discretion to enter a subsequent order requiring that all future cases be processed in criminal court. However, the juvenile court has the discretion to vacate this order at any time (Szymanski, 2011).

One last area in which laws may differ concerns whether the transfer provision can be applied to a juvenile who has previously been tried and convicted as an adult in another jurisdiction or state (Szymanski, 2011). Kansas law, for example, states, "The definition of juvenile offender excludes anyone who has previously been . . . convicted or sentenced as an adult under the laws of another state or country with transfer procedures comparable to those of Kansas" (Kan. Stat. Ann. § 38-2302(s)(3)). Mississippi and Oklahoma have similar laws, which recognize the certification of a juvenile as an adult in other states (Miss. Code Ann. § 43-21-157(8); Okla. Stat. Ann. tit. 10A § 2-5-204(G)(1)-(2)).

THE BENEFITS AND DRAWBACKS OF ONCE AN ADULT/ALWAYS AN ADULT LAWS

Both positive and negative aspects of once an adult, always an adult law have been identified (Pegg, 2015). One proposed benefit concerns the protection of non-transferred youth housed in the juvenile justice system. Researchers have found that juveniles who have been housed in adult facilities as a result of transfer often adopt procriminal or antisocial values that they learned while in adult facilities (Eisikovits & Baizerman, 1982; Woodard et al., 2005). If transferred juveniles who have previously been incarcerated with adult individuals were to be returned to juvenile court jurisdiction for subsequent offenses and placed in juvenile facilities with non-transferred youth, they may bring their newly learned criminal habits and values to juvenile detention centers, thus potentially impacting the ability to rehabilitate non-transferred youth (Mays & Ruddell, 2012). Therefore, by making transferred youth ineligible for processing in juvenile court jurisdiction, non-transferred youth in juvenile detention centers may be protected from the more serious and advanced juvenile offenders.

Another benefit of once an adult, always an adult law is that juveniles processed in the adult court gain more due process rights. During the 1950s and 1960s, confidence in the juvenile court's ability to rehabilitate juvenile offenders began to waiver (Snyder & Sickmund, 1999). Recognizing that the juvenile system was not living up to its primary purpose of rehabilitating youthful offenders, the Supreme Court issued a series of rulings to provide juveniles with more protections (*Breed v. Jones*, 1975; *In re Gault*, 1967; *In re Winship*, 1970). Believing that juveniles were not receiving the necessary treatment promised by the juvenile court, the Supreme Court ruled they should at least be granted some due process rights. The Supreme Court granted juveniles many of the same due process protections as adults, but stopped short of granting them all the same protections. Specifically, the Court failed to grant juveniles the right to a trial by jury in *McKeiver v. Pennsylvania* (1971). Additionally, the Court has failed to make a ruling regarding whether juveniles have a constitutional right to bail; thus, many states either explicitly prohibit its use or simply neither authorize or prohibit its use (National Juvenile Defender Center, 2019). As of 2019, only eighteen states grant the use of bail for juveniles processed in juvenile court.

Given that juveniles processed in juvenile court are not granted all the same due process protections of adults, being transferred to the adult system does have the added benefit of gaining more due process protections (Pegg, 2015). A transferred juvenile is now able to receive a jury trial as opposed to having their case handled by a single juvenile court judge. Similarly, juveniles who may have previously been held in detention upon waiting for their trial if processed in the juvenile court may now have the opportunity to seek bail and be granted release prior to their trial. Ultimately, previously transferred youth who are automatically transferred to adult court as a result of once an adult, always an adult law enjoy the benefit of more due process rights than they would have received if they had remained within the juvenile court.

While once an adult, always adult laws may have some positive aspects, the doctrine has received substantial criticism. One such criticism stems from the fact that the provision requires an automatic waiver (Pegg, 2015). By automatically waiving juveniles previously processed in adult court, there is no consideration of potentially important mitigating factors, such as age of the offender, possibility of rehabilitation, culpability, or psychological development, that may bring to light a reason for handling the juvenile within the juvenile justice system (Szymanski, 2011). Depending on the transfer laws of the state in which the juvenile committed the crime, it is possible that a juvenile may be initially transferred to adult court without ever receiving a hearing where culpability and amenability to treatment are assessed (Pegg, 2015). For example, if a sixteen-year-old commits a rape (Class A felony) in the state of Alabama, he would be charged, arrested, and tried as an adult, without any culpability hearing, due to the state's statutory exclusion law (Ala. Code § 12-15-204). After conviction, if said juvenile were to commit any future criminal acts, regardless of the severity, the juvenile would automatically be tried as an adult (Ala. Code § 12-15-204(b)). Thus, a juvenile could forever be bound to the adult court without ever having their psychological development, culpability, amenability to treatment, life history, and so on assessed by the court.

Once an adult/always an adult law is also challenged on the grounds that they are being applied to more juvenile offenders than which was originally intended. Once an adult/always an adult law, as well as transfer laws more generally, was designed to remove serious, repeat offenders from the jurisdiction of the juvenile court. However, research has found that there have been many transfers of nonviolent offenders. According to data from the Office of Juvenile Justice and Delinquency Prevention, during the period of 1985–2008, 60.5 percent of youth transferred to adult court had committed a nonviolent offense (Sickmund et al., 2011; as cited in Mays & Ruddell, 2012). Thus, in states where all that is required for the once an adult, always an adult provision to be applied is a conviction in adult court and the commission of a subsequent offense, there can be nonviolent juvenile offenders forever bound to the adult court jurisdiction, thus ignoring their amenability to treatment as well as limiting their likelihood of receiving appropriate rehabilitative services.

As discussed previously, once an adult, always an adult law was not designed with rehabilitation in mind. Rather, the purpose was to hold juvenile offenders accountable and increase public safety by deterring future criminal behavior (Clarke, 2005). However, some research suggests that once an adult, always an adult law is not achieving this intended goal. In fact, there is some evidence that suggests that such laws are having a criminogenic effect (Lanza-Kaduce et al., 2005). Though the evidence is somewhat mixed, studies have found that transferred youth are more likely to recidivate than similarly situated juveniles processed in juvenile courts. For example, in a natural experiment on the deterrent effects of juvenile versus adult court sanctions, Fagan and colleagues (Fagan, 1996; Kupchik et al., 2003) found that transfer was associated with a greater likelihood of, and quicker time to, rearrests for robbery offenders. Similarly, in their study of adult felony recidivism for 475 matched pairs of juveniles processed in either the juvenile or adult court, Lanza-Kaduce and colleagues (2005) found that even after controlling for case details, transferred youth were more likely to reoffend and more likely to commit violence after they turned eighteen. Once an adult/always an adult law, and other transfer laws, failure to deter future offending may stem from the fact that juveniles are developmentally immature. This leads to another criticism of once an adult, always an adult law: their failure to recognize the biological and social realities of youth (Pegg, 2015).

Neurological research has found that there is a biological basis for youth's immaturity and risk-taking behavior (Walsh, 2011). The frontal lobes of the brain—the portion of the brain responsible for judgment and impulse control—do not finish developing until individuals have well passed their teenage years (Mays & Ruddell, 2012). Therefore, it is argued that juveniles "do not yet possess the full biological capacity to understand or control attraction to risky irresponsible behavior" (Pegg, 2015, p. 150). Juveniles may then continue to engage in criminal behavior despite the possible punishments due to their lack of impulse control and poor decision-making skills that result from developmental immaturity. Given this knowledge, once an adult, always an adult law is likely to have little impact on future behavior, as evidenced by the research, because juveniles are experiencing a "maturity gap."

A final criticism of once an adult, always an adult law concerns the deleterious effects that transferred youth experience as a result of being placed in adult correctional institutions. Federal law prohibits juveniles from being held in adult correctional institutions (Campaign for Youth Justice, 2007). Specifically, the Juvenile Justice and Delinquency Prevention Act (1974) states juveniles "will not be detained or confined in any institution in which they have contact with adult inmates." However, there is a caveat. Juveniles who are transferred to adult court lose their "juvenile" status and thus become exempt from this prohibition (Pegg, 2015). Though limited, there is some research to suggest that youth held in adult facilities are at an increased risk of physical or sexual victimization (Beyer, 1997; Redding, 1999). Beyer (1997), for example, found that juveniles in adult correctional facilities were more likely to be both beaten by staff and sexually assaulted than juveniles held in juvenile institutions.

Placement of youth in an adult facility also has an impact on their mental health. The Campaign for Youth Justice (2007) reports that youth in adult jails are nineteen times more likely to commit suicide than their counterparts in the general population. Part of their explanation of this finding is that adult correctional facilities are simply not equipped to identify and respond to the mental health needs of youthful offenders.

CONCLUSION

The current era of juvenile justice seems to be moving away from the "get tough" policies of the past several decades back toward more child-focused policies (Benekos & Merlo, 2019). Evidence of this shift in ideology can be seen in recent Supreme Court rulings that restrict excessive juvenile punishments (see *Roper v. Simmons, Graham v. Florida, Miller v. Alabama, and Montgomery v. Louisiana*) as well as in policies that acknowledge the impact of trauma on criminal behavior (Abram et al., 2013; Listenbee, 2014; U.S. Department of Justice, 2010;) and the importance of relevant treatment (e.g., trauma-informed approach) (Listenbee et al., 2012). Given these new developments, it will be interesting to see whether states decide to either revise or repeal their once an adult, always an adult laws. As noted earlier, some states have been successful in reforming their laws to limit the scope to whom the law can be applied (Neelum, 2011). However, to date, only one state has been successful in completely repealing the law. Perhaps with the current developments in juvenile justice along with the acknowledgment that once an adult, always an adult laws are not achieving their intended purpose, further reform will take place aimed at modifying these types of automatic transfer laws and removing more juveniles from the throws of the criminal justice system.

REFERENCES

Abram, K. M., Teplin, L. A., King, D. C., Longworth, S. L., Emanuel, K. M., Romero, E. G., McClelland, G. M., Dulcan, M. K., Washburn, J. J., Welty, L.

J., & Olson, N. D. (2013). *PTSD, trauma, and comorbid psychiatric disorders in detained youth.* U.S. Department of Justice, Office of Justice Programs, Office of Juvenile Justice and Delinquency Prevention.

Benekos, P. J., & Merlo, A. V. (2019). A decade of change: Roper v. Simmons, Defending Childhood, and juvenile justice policy. *Criminal Justice Policy Review, 30*(1), 102–127.

Bennett, W. J., Dilulio, J. J., & Walters, J. P. (1996). *Body count: Moral poverty and how to win America's war against crime and drugs.* Simon and Schuster.

Beyer, M. (1997). Experts for juveniles at risk of adult sentences. In P. Puritz, A. Capozello, & W. Shang (Eds.), *More than meets the eye: Rethinking assessment, competency and sentencing for a harsher era of juvenile justice* (pp. 1–22). American Bar Association Juvenile Justice Center.

Breed v. Jones, 421 U.S. 519 (1975).

Butts, J. A., & Travis, J. (2002). *The rise and fall of American youth violence: 1980 to 2000.* Urban Institute.

Campaign for Youth Justice (2007). *Jailing juveniles: The dangers of incarcerating youth in adult jails in America.* http://www.campaignforyouthjustice.org/Downloads/NationalReportsArticles/CFYJ-Jailing_Juveniles_Report_2007-11-15.pdf

Clarke, C. (2005). The baby and the bathwater: Adolescent offending and punitive juvenile justice reform. *University of Kansas Law Review, 53*(3), 659–726.

DiIulio, J. J. (1995). The coming of the super-predators. *The Weekly Standard, 1*, 23.

Eisikovits, Z., & Baiserman, M. L. (1982). "Doin time": Violent youth in a juvenile facility and in an adult prison. *Journal of Offender Counseling Services Rehabilitation, 6*(3), 5–20.

Fagan, J. (1996). The comparative advantage of juvenile versus criminal court sanctions on recidivism among adolescent felony offenders. *Law & Policy, 18*, 77–112.

Garcia, M. (2015, December 31). New Illinois laws aim to keep teens out of prison system. *Chicago Tribune.* https://www.chicagotribune.com/politics/ct-illinois-juvenile-justice-new-laws-met-20151230-story.html

Griffin, P. (2008). *Different from adults: An updated analysis of juvenile transfer and blended sentencing laws, with recommendations for reform.* National Center for Juvenile Justice.

Griffin, P., Addie, S., Adams, B., & Firestine, K. (2011). *Trying juveniles as adults: An analysis of transfer laws and reporting.* Office of Juvenile Justice and Delinquency Prevention.

Griffin, P., Torbet, P., & Szymanksi, L. (1998). *Trying juveniles as adults in criminal court: An analysis of state transfer provisions.* Office of Juvenile Justice and Delinquency Prevention.

H.B. 3007, 2007 Gen. Assem., Reg. Sess. (Va. 2007).

H.E. 1122, 115th Gen. Assem., 2d Reg. Sess. (Ind. 2008)

In re Gault, 387 U.S. 1 (1967).

In re Winship, 397 U.S. 358 (1970).

Juvenile Jurisdiction Advisory Committee (2019). *Juvenile jurisdiction advisory committee (S.L. 2017-57): Juvenile age interim report.* https://files.nc.gov/ncdps/documents/files/JJAC_Jan_15_report_Complete.pdf

Juvenile Justice and Delinquency Prevention Act (1974).

Juvenile Justice Geography, Policy, Practice & Statistics (n.d.). *Jurisdictional boundaries.* http://www.jjgps.org/jurisdictional-boundaries

Kupchick, A., Fagan, J., & Liberman, A. (2003). Punishment, proportionality, and jurisdictional transfer of adolescent offenders: A test of the leniency gap hypothesis. *Stanford Law and Policy Review, 14*, 57–83.

Lanza-Kaduce, L., Lane, J., Bishop, D. M., & Frazier, C. E. (2005). Juvenile offenders and adult felony recidivism: The impact of transfer. *Journal of Crime and Justice, 28*(1), 59–77.

Listenbee, R. L. (2014, June 9). *The juvenile justice and delinquency prevention act: Preserving potential, protecting communities.* Testimony before the Committee on the Judiciary U.S. Senate (Field Hearing, Pawtucket, RI). http://www.judiciary.senate.gov/imo/media/doc/06-09-14ListenbeeTestimony.pdf

Listenbee, R. L., Torre, J., Boyle, G., Cooper, S. W., Deer, S., Durfee, D. T., James, T., Lieberman, A., Macy, R., Marans, S. McDonnell, J., Mendoza, G., & Taguba, A. (2012). *Defending childhood: Report of the attorney general's national task force on children exposed to violence.* U.S. Department of Justice, Office of Juvenile Justice and Delinquency Prevention, Office of Justice Programs. https://www.justice.gov/sites/default/files/defendingchildhood/legacy/2012/12/12/cev-executive-sum.pdf

Mays, G. L., & Ruddell, R. (2012). *Do the crime, do the time: Juvenile criminals and adult justice in the American court system.* Praeger.

McKeiver v. Pennsylvania, 403 U.S. 528 (1971).

Merlo, A. V., Benekos, P. J., & Cook, W. J. (1999). The juvenile court at 100 years: Celebration or wake. *Juvenile and Family Court Journal, 50*(3), 1–10.

National Juvenile Defender Center. (2018). *State profiles.* https://njdc.info/practice-policy-resources/state-profiles/

National Juvenile Defender Center. (2019). A right to liberty: Juvenile cash bail reform. https://njdc.info/our-work/juvenile-bail-reform/

Neelum, A. (2011). *State trends: Legislative changes from 2005 to 2010: Removing youth from the adult criminal justice system.* Washington, DC: Campaign for Youth Justice.

Nevada Legislature's Legislative Committee on Child Welfare and Juvenile Justice's Task Force to Study Juvenile Justice Issues (2014). Summary minutes and action report. https://www.leg.state.nv.us/App/InterimCommittee/REL/Interim2013/Meeting/4660

Pegg, K. (2015). The "Once an Adult, Always an Adult" doctrine: More harm than good. *Indiana Journal of Law and Social Equality, 3*(1), 144–160.

Redding, R. E. (1999). Examining legal issues: Juvenile offenders in criminal and adult prison. *Corrections Today, 61*(2): 92–124.

S.S.B. No. 5746, 60th Leg., Reg., Sess. (Wash. 2009).

Snyder, H. N., & Sickmund, M. (1999). *Juvenile justice: A century of change.* Office of Juvenile Justice and Delinquency Prevention.

Szymanski, L. A. (2002). "Once an Adult, Always and Adult" (2001 Update) and juvenile can request transfer to criminal court. *NCJJ Snapshot, 7*(7). National Center for Juvenile Justice.

Szymanski, L. A. (2011). Once a juvenile is transferred to criminal court must they be tried as adults for all future offenses? *NCJJ Snapshot, 16*(9). National Center for Juvenile Justice.

Torbet, P., & Szymanski, L. (1998). *State legislative responses to violent juvenile crime: 1996–97 Update.* Office of Juvenile Justice and Delinquency Prevention, Department of Justice.

U.S. Department of Justice. (2010). *Defending childhood: Protect, heal, thrive: Fact sheet.* http://www.justice.gov/ag/defendingchildhood/dc-factsheet.pdf

Walsh, C. (2011). Youth justice and neuroscience: A dual-use dilemma. *British Journal of Criminology, 51*(1), 21–39.

Woolard, J. L., Odgers, C., Lanza-Kaduce, L., & Daglis, H. (2005). Juveniles within adult correctional settings: Legal pathways and developmental considerations. *The International Journal of Forensic Mental Health, 4*(1), 1–18.

Zimring, F. E. (1998). *American youth violence.* Oxford University Press.

Chapter 5

Waiver in Use

Sheri Jenkins Keenan

JUDICIAL WAIVER

All of the waiver mechanisms are accompanied by a host of strengths and weaknesses. For example, the literature reflects many concerns about judicial waiver, including the belief that judges are vested with too much discretion, and the belief that race influences the waiver decision (Burrow, 2008; Clarke, 1996; Fagan, Forest, & Vivona, 1987). Some research suggests similarly situated juvenile offenders receiving "adult time" (Burrow, 2008, p. 34), vary for a variety of reasons (Burrow, 2008; Kurlycheck & Johnson, 2004; Myers, 2003; van Vleet, 1999).

Judicial waiver has been tracked for several years, but cases waived by prosecutorial direct file or statutory exclusion are not systematically examined (Griffin, Addie, Adams, & Firestine, 2011; McCord, Widom, & Crowell, 2001; Fagan, 2008). Waivers by juvenile judges have remained fairly constant between 1986 to 1996, representing between 1 percent and 1.6 percent of all petitioned cases (Lawrence & Hemmens, 2008; McCord et al., 2001; Sickmund et al., 1998; Snyder & Sickmund, 1999; Stahl, Finnegan, & Kang, 2007, 2002). There is some evidence that a similar percentage of cases were waived in the early years of the juvenile court (McCord et al., 2001). About 1 percent of cases were waived by the Milwaukee Juvenile Court in the early twentieth century (Schlossman, 1977). In a study of the Chicago juvenile court, Jeter (1922) reported that the percentage of boys waived to adult criminal court per year was usually less than 1 percent.

Some evidence suggests that at least as many if not more juveniles are sent into the adult criminal justice system via these other two methods (Bilchik, 1999, 1998; Butts & Harrell, 1998; Fagan, 2008; Lawrence & Hemmens, 2008). In 1995, Florida waived close to 7,000 juveniles to the adult criminal court; the bulk of these juveniles were waived using direct file (Jordan & Freiburg, 2010; Jordan & Myers, 2011; Lawrence & Hemmens, 2008; Mears, 2003; Mears & Butts, 2008). In that same year, 9,700 juveniles were waived to the adult criminal court via judicial waiver; thus, Florida's nonjudicial waiver alone almost matched the nation's total number of judicial waiver (Sickmund et al., 1998).

In 2007, data reported to the National Juvenile Court Data Archive indicated that 8,500 juveniles were waived using the judicial waiver (Griffin et al., 2011). Arizona, California, Florida, Michigan, Oregon, and Washington reported an additional 5,096 nonjudicial waiver cases (Griffin et al., 2011).

Despite some stability in the overall proportion of cases waived via judicial waiver, there is variety by type of offense. Between 1986 and 1996, cases involving crimes against persons— homicide, rape, robbery, aggravated assault, simple assault, and other violent sex offense—were the most likely to be sent to the adult criminal court by juvenile court judges; about 2 percent of person offense cases resulted in judicial waiver (Sickmund et al., 1998; Stahl et al., 1999). In the late 1980s, there was a dramatic increase in waiver for drug offense cases, which increased from 1.2 percent in 1986 to 4.1 percent in 1991 (McCord et al., 2001). By the mid-1990, the percentage of drug offenses waived dropped back down to 1.2 percent (McCord et al., 2001). The peak occurred during the height of the war on drugs, which lead to a rise in youth violence (McCord et al., 2001). Waiver decisions may have been influenced by the general antidrug campaign of the period.

In an analysis of judicial waiver decisions in Boston, Detroit, Newark, and Phoenix between 1981 and 1984, Fagan et al. (1987) found that age at the time of offense was committed, age of delinquency onset, and seriousness of offense were the factors that most influenced juvenile judges' decisions to waive a case to criminal court. As one might expect, juveniles who are waived to the adult criminal court end to be older and charged with serious violent offenses, most usually homicide.

Studies in Virginia (Poulos & Orchowsky, 1994) and New Mexico (Houghtalin & Mays, 1991) examined the factors influencing judicial waiver between 1988 and 1990. They found that the factors most important to juvenile judges' decisions to waive a case included current offense, prior record, and age. Most likely to be waived were juveniles who were charged with homicide, rape, drug sales, older juveniles, juveniles who used a gun in committing the offense, and those with prior felony person or drug adjudications or prior commitment to a residential juvenile correctional faculty. Judges in larger cities were less likely to waive cases than were those in rural counties.

Podkopacz and Feld (1996) analyzed judicial waiver motions filed between 1986 and 1992 in Hennepin County, Minnesota, and determined that in addition to age, present offense, and weapon use, the recommendation of probation officers and clinical evaluators significantly affected the judicial waiver decision. They also found prior correctional interventions to be significant. Juveniles with no prior program placements and those with only a few; one to three, were less likely to be waived to the adult criminal court than juveniles with four or more placements.

DIRECT FILE

National data on the number of cases waived through direct file are not available (National Research Council, 2000) and there is far less research on direct file (Bishop, 2000; Bishop & Frazier, 1991, 1996; Burrow, 2008; Thomas & Bilchik, 1985). Direct file allows the prosecutors to determine where the juvenile will be prosecuted, that is, juvenile court or adult criminal court (Griffin et al., 2011). This charging discretion is important for two reasons. First, prosecutors are not required to consider the best interest of the child (Burrow, 2008; Feld, 1991). Second, public safety becomes the dominant concern (Bishop, Frazier, & Henretta, 1989). Nonetheless, a number of questions have been raised about direct file.

In contrast to the findings regarding judicial waiver, Bishop and Frazier (1991) found that juveniles waived via direct file in Florida from 1979 to 1981 were not violent or chronic offenders; 55 percent of those waived were felony property offenses and only 29 percent were felony person offense.

McCarthy (1994) focused on whether direct file is necessary to avoid extreme outcomes in case processing. Similarly, Davis (2000) suggested that direct file may largely be an overreaction to a "phantom menace." Other concerns have focused on the fact that the charging decisions of prosecutors are not reviewable which makes it unclear whether the most serious offenders are being charged and whether some offenders should be charged as adults at all (Feld, 2004; Sabo, 1996; Sanborn, 2003). Although the research shows that there are differences of opinion with respect to the efficacy of direct file, there is mounting evidence that it may be the least favored method of addressing serious juvenile offending (Bishop, 2004; Bishop, Lanza-Kaduce, & Frazier, 1998; Boyce, 1994; Burrow, 2008; Cintron, 1996).

The 1994 National Survey of Prosecutors (DeFrances & Strom, 1997) conducted by the Bureau of Justice Statistics sampled 308 chief prosecutors nationwide from the 2,343 who try felony cases in state courts. Among prosecutors' offices nationwide, 94 percent reported handling one or more types of juvenile cases. Over 80 percent of all offices handled juvenile delinquency cases and requests to waive juveniles to adult criminal court. Among offices handling juvenile cases, 63 percent reported they had waived at least one juvenile case to adult criminal court in 1994. Ninety-six percent of large full-time offices reported handling waiver to adult criminal court, compared to 67 percent of small, full-time offices, and 48 percent of part-time offices. Among offices handling juvenile cases, about 19 percent had a specialized unit that dealt with juvenile cases waived to adult criminal court. These specialized units were most often found in large, full-time offices; 61 percent. The types of cases waived varied by type of office. In full-time offices in large jurisdictions, 80 percent of the offices reported that at least one murder case was waived and 72 percent reported at least one robbery case. Sixty percent of part-time offices handling juvenile cases waived to adult criminal court reported that at least one burglary case was waived.

A study by the U.S. General Accounting Office (1995) based on data from five states and the District of Columbia found that the percentage of cases sent to adult criminal court by prosecutorial direct file ranged from less than 1 percent (Utah) to 10 percent (Florida) to 13 percent (Arkansas). In some states, the change to prosecutorial direct file has increased the number of juveniles that have been sent to the adult criminal court (McCord et al., 2001).

STATUTORY EXCLUSION

Recent changes in statutory exclusion laws have generally increased the population of juveniles potentially subject to waive to the adult criminal courts, but no national data are currently available to determine the actual number of juveniles affected by exclusion laws, the characteristics of such juveniles, or the offenses for which they are waived. A 1985 study of twelve jurisdictions reported that juveniles waived by statutory exclusion tended to be younger and to have fewer prior arrests and placements than juveniles waived by other means (Gragg, 1986).

Clarke (1996), in a study of statutory exclusion waiver in Cook County, Illinois, from 1992 to 1994, found that 39 percent of the waiver were for drug or weapon offense, 25 percent were for murder, and 22 percent were for armed robbery. The proportion of waiver cases for murder had dropped from nearly half of those waived by judicial waiver from 1975 to 1981 to a quarter under statutory exclusion. Clarke (1996) concluded that Illinois's statutory exclusion provisions failed to identify and therefore protect the public against serious violent juvenile offenders. Instead, they prosecuted and stigmatized many juveniles who did not represent a threat to public safety and who could benefit from the more rehabilitative programs of the juvenile court.

THE EFFECTS OF WAIVER

Juveniles waived to the adult criminal court are more likely to be convicted of both the target charge and reduced charges than juveniles processed in juvenile court (Coalition for Juvenile Justice, 2005; Lanza-Kaduce, Lane, Bishop, & Frazier, 2005). The processing of a juvenile who has been waived to the adult criminal court from time of waiver to the sentencing phase takes more than twice as long as the adjudication process in juvenile court and those who are incarcerated experience longer periods of confinement (Coalition for Juvenile Justice, 2005). There are fewer treatment opportunities; schooling vocational training, and mental health, for juveniles who are incarcerated in the adult facilities verses those juveniles who are held in juvenile correctional facilities (Coalition for Juvenile Justice, 2005; Podkopacz & Feld, 1996). Juveniles waived to the adult criminal court are more likely to recidivate, with more serious offenses, and with a shorter survival rate than juveniles who are prosecuted through the juvenile court system (Coalition for Juvenile Justice, 2005; Myers, 2003, 2005; Podkopacz & Feld, 1996). Juveniles who are incarcerated in adult prisons face high rates of victimization, particularly violence and sexual assault, then juveniles who are sent to juvenile facilities (Coalition for Juvenile Justice, 2005). The following research bears this out.

Deterrence

During the past thirty-five years, policymakers, driven by the public concerns and fears of crime, have supported various get-tough strategies. The more popular approaches have included three strikes and you're out, truth in sentencing provisions, expanded use of the death penalty, boot camps, juvenile waiver, and stricter law enforcement. The foundation of these measures is a belief in the value of increased retribution and incapacitation. They are also supported based on the idea that punishment deters criminal and delinquent behavior.

Waiving juveniles to the adult criminal court corresponds well with this view. Supporters of this practice contend that adult criminal court is the appropriate place for juvenile offenders who exhibit serious and violent criminal behavior (Fagan, 1996; Myers, 2003). It is asserted that in adult criminal court, a message can be sent that lenient treatment of the juvenile system is no longer an option (Bishop, Frazier, Lanza-Kaduce, & Winner, 1996; Myers, 2003, 2005). Instead, harsh adult criminal court sanctions will be imposed, which will increase public safety and reduce motivations to commit future crimes. In sum, adult criminal court is believed to provide stronger punishment and deterrence. These underlying beliefs suggest that the effectiveness of treating juvenile offenders as adults is based on the nature of the punishment it produces; certain, severe, and swift (Beccaria, 1764; Butts & Mitchell, 2000; Lawrence & Hemmens, 2008; Myers, 2005; Redding, 2008).

The research on the deterrent effects of waiving juveniles to the adult criminal court is decidedly mixed. Some studies identify lower recidivism rates, some higher, and some no difference (Griffin et al., 2011; Mears, 2003). The idea that waiver can actually result in greater rates of recidivism generates a concern because such an outcome clearly suggests a problem with the use of waiver (Mears, 2003). Some studies (Bishop et al., 1996; Fagan, 1995; Podkopacz & Feld, 1996; Winner, Lanza-Kaduce, Bishop, & Frazier, 1997) suggest that recidivism rates are higher among juveniles who have been waived to the adult criminal court. These studies (Bishop et al., 1996; Fagan, 1995; Podkopacz & Feld, 1996; Winner et al., 1997) suggest a number of reasons for the higher recidivism rates, including the correct identification of juveniles likely to recidivate, increased vigilance by law enforcement to juveniles with adult records, and being incarcerated with adults may have encouraged further criminality.

Before the widespread expansion of waiver laws, Glassner, Ksander, Berg, and Johnson (1983) reported the results of interviews with juvenile offenders in New York. These juvenile offenders indicated they had decided to stop offending once they reached the age at which they knew they could be tried as adults.

Studies from New York (Singer & McDowall, 1988) and Idaho (Jensen & Metsger, 1994) suggest waiving juveniles to the adult criminal court does not have a deterrent effect on violent juvenile crime. Singer and McDowall (1988) evaluated New York's statutory exclusion law. The statutory exclusion law became effective in 1978 and lowered the age at which juveniles could be waived to thirteen for murder and fourteen for assault, arson, burglary, kidnapping, and rape. Using Philadelphia data for comparison purposes, the authors conducted trend analysis of monthly juvenile violent crime arrest rates during the period of 1974 to 1984. Singer and McDowall (1988) found that the new statutory exclusion law did not produce the expected deterrent effect.

In Idaho, Jensen and Metsger (1994) evaluated their state's statutory exclusion law (1981) that required violent juvenile offenders from age fourteen to eighteen to be sent to the adult criminal court. Jensen and Mesger (1994) used Montana and Wyoming as comparison states. Jensen and Metsger (1994) found that the statutory exclusion law had no deterrent effect on violent juvenile crime.

Similar results were found by Bishop (1996) et al., in their Florida study with the additional finding that in some cases recidivism of juvenile waived to the adult criminal court involved more serious crimes; 93 percent of waived juveniles who were rearrested were charged with a felony, while 85 percent of the retained juveniles who were rearrested were charged with a felony. In a six-year follow-up to the Florida study, researchers found that waiving juveniles to the adult criminal court led to more recidivism (Winner et al., 1997).

In their study of juveniles considered for waiver in Hennepin County, Minnesota, Podkopacz and Feld (1996) also failed to find evidence of greater deterrence in waiving juveniles to the adult criminal court. During a two-year follow-up period, 58 percent of the waived offenders were convicted of a new crime in contrast to only 42 percent of the retained juveniles. The authors offered three possible explanations for the lower juvenile court recidivism rate. First, through an emphasis on prior offending, the juvenile court succeeded in waiving the most serious and frequent offenders who had a greater probability of recidivism. Next, treatment services were more effective in the juvenile correctional system. Finally, the adult criminal system better trained rather than deterred further criminality than did the juvenile system.

Risler, Sweatman, and Nackerud (1998) subsequently assessed the general deterrent effects of Georgia's 1994 legislative waiver law. Juvenile arrest rates were again compared before and after implementation of the new law. Analysis of the 1992 to 1995 data indicated that there were no significant reductions in arrest rates for the specified waiver offenses, suggesting that the law did not reduce serious juvenile crime.

Levitt (1998) in his study examined the punitiveness of the juvenile court and adult criminal court on arrest rates. Levitt (1998) found that in states in which the adult criminal court was more punitive than the juvenile court, violent crime rates decreased at the age of majority. This suggests that the punitiveness of the state adult criminal court rather than waiver reduces recidivism.

Myers (2003, 2005) and Myers and Kiehl (2001) in their research on 557 violent juvenile offenders processed in Pennsylvania juvenile and adult criminal courts in 1994 found evidence of greater recidivism among waived juveniles during both the pre-dispositional and post-dispositional states of processing. Of the 224 offenders who were released from pre-dispositional secure custody, those in adult court were more likely to be rearrested and also exhibited more serious pre-dispositional recidivism compared with their counterparts in juvenile court. Similarly, during an eighteen-month post-dispositional follow-up period, the waived juveniles displayed greater, more serious, and faster recidivism than did offenders retained in juvenile court, while controlling for a variety of offense and offender characteristics. These findings support those of previous studies that found no evidence of a deterrent effect from juvenile waiver to adult criminal court.

In Georgia, Redding and Fuller (2004) interviewed juvenile offenders who had been charged with murder or armed robbery and had automatically been tried as adults. Redding and Fuller (2004) found that despite increased publicity on the new automatic waiver law, juveniles were not deterred. Many of the juveniles reported thinking they would only get light sentences from the juvenile court such as probation, boot camp, several months in juvenile detention.

In Florida between 1989 and 2002, Lee and McCrary (2005), evaluated the effects of turning eighteen on criminal offending. They found that juveniles did not lower their offending rates upon turning eighteen. This suggests that the prospect of adult criminal court sanctions was not a deterrent.

Macan and Rees (2005) examined delinquency data for drug selling assault, robbery, burglary and theft from the 1995 National Longitudinal Study of Adolescent Health. They found that the arrest rate had only a general deterrent effect on the crimes of drug dealing and assault.

Steiner and Wright (2006) examined the effects of prosecutorial waiver laws in fourteen states. The study found that the prosecutorial waiver law had no general deterrent effect on juvenile crime.

Griffin et al. (2011) warn in their article that blanket statements about waiver deterring juvenile crime should be read with caution. Furthermore, they assert that several decades of research has generally failed to establish that waiver laws deter juvenile crime and or reduce further criminal behavior (Griffin et al., 2011).

Recidivism

There have been several major studies that have been conducted to examine whether the waiving of a juvenile to the adult criminal court reduces individual recidivism, specific deterrence. These studies indicate that juveniles tried in adult criminal court have greater recidivism rates after release than those tried in juvenile court. Prior to these major studies research was mixed on rates of recidivism for juvenile offenders. For example, Smith and Gartin (1989) found that being arrested reduced recidivism among first time, male offenders.

Fagan (1996) examined the recidivism rates of juvenile offenders charged with robbery or burglary in New Jersey and New York. The study found that adult criminal court processing produces a higher recidivism rate. Mason and Chang (2001) in their study found similar findings; processing juveniles through the adult criminal court had a substantially higher recidivism rate than juveniles processed through the juvenile court.

In Florida, Bishop et al. (1996) compared recidivism rates juvenile offenders waived to adult criminal court. Researchers found that the rearrest rates were higher, and the average time to reoffend shorter among waived juveniles.

A seven-year follow-up study by Winner et al. (1997) found that the rearrest rates were higher and the time to reoffending shorter among juveniles who had been waived to the adult criminal court; the exception was waived property felons.

Bishop and Frazier (2000) found that juveniles processed in the adult system view the waiver experience as punitive, uncaring, and unfair, whereas juveniles processed in the juvenile justice system typically feel that various court actors care about and are fair in their treatment of them. These perceptions of unfairness might potentially contribute to increased recidivism (Sherman and Weisberg, 1995). It also is possible that experiences in adult prisons, including poorer adjustment and a greater risk of victimization than would occur in juvenile facilities, may affect subsequent criminal behavior (Maitland & Sluder, 1998; McShane & Williams, 1989).

In Pennsylvania, Myers (2001) examined the recidivism rates of juvenile offenders charged with robbery or aggravated assault. Researchers found that juveniles who were judicially waived to the adult criminal court were more likely to be rearrested, and in a shorter amount of time.

In Colorado, Cohen, Glackman, and Odgers (2003) studied serious juveniles offenders incarcerated in a maximum-security facility. The researchers found a negative relationship between the juveniles' sentence severity and self-reported intent to reoffend. In addition, the researchers found a positive correlation between their self-report intent to reoffend, and the number of offenses they actually committed after their release.

Lanza-Kaduce et al. (2005) conducted a study in Florida that included young adult offenders; half of the offenders had been prosecutorial waived, and the other half had remained in the juvenile court. The researchers found that waived juvenile was significantly more likely to reoffend. Lanza-Kaduce et al. (2005) stated the following conclusion:

> Overall, 49% of the waived juvenile offenders reoffended, compared with 35% of the retained offenders. For violent offenses, 24% of the waived offenders reoffended, compared with 16% of the retained offenders. For drug offenses, 11% of the waived offenders reoffended, compared with 9% of the retained offender and for property offenses, 14% of the waived offenders reoffended, compared with 10% of the retained offenders. The results were virtually identical for the subset of 315 best matched pairs. (Lanza-Kaduce et al., 2005, p. 136)

Increased Victimization

Juveniles who receive the punishment of incarceration in the adult criminal court usually serve their sentences in adult prisons and jails. More than 6,500 juveniles were being held in adult jails as of June 1998 (Forst et al. 1989). Juveniles in adult correctional facilities suffer higher rates of physical abuse, sexual abuse, and suicide (Forst et al. 1989; Young

& Gainsborough, 2000). In a study conducted by Forst et al. (1989), the researchers found that compared to those held in juvenile detention centers, juveniles held in adult jails are "7.7 times more likely to commit suicide, 5 times more likely to be sexually assaulted, 2 times more likely to be beaten by correctional staff, and 50 percent more likely to be attacked with a weapon" (p. 56).

Similarly, studies by McShane and Williams (1989) and Maitland and Sluder (1998) also reveal that juveniles in adult prisons are more likely to be victimized and to experience more difficult transitions to incarceration.

The victimization of juveniles waived to the adult criminal court is an undesirable outcome. Lawrence and Hemmens (2008) note that juvenile victimization in adult correctional facilities has a potentially negative effect on prison control and successful transitions back into society. They also note that the physical abuse, sexual abuse, and suicide as well as other additional concerns, once an adult always an adult statute, conviction a matter of public record, disclosure of past criminal activity to future employers, voting rights, and right to serve in the military have been largely unaddressed by waiver research (Lawrence & Hemmens, 2008).

Net Widening

Net widening is used to describe the effects of providing alternatives to incarceration, that is, diversion programs, to direct juvenile offenders away from juvenile court. While diversion programs were originally intended to reduce the numbers of juveniles in lock up facilities or reduce the numbers going to juvenile court, scholars suggest that what has happened instead is that the total numbers of offenders under the control of the state have increased. Clearly, net widening has occurred (Butts & Mitchell, 2000; Lawrence & Hemmens, 2008; Myers, 2001).

Few researchers have examined the extent to which net widening results from waiver laws because waiver is typically thought of as being used for the more serious, chronic, and violent offenders (Butts & Mitchell, 2000; Lawrence & Hemmens, 2008; Myers, 2001). However, in contrast to the stated goals in many state statutes, waivers are frequently used for less serious property and drug offenders. Applied such cases, net widening becomes a very real possibility (Butts and Mitchell, 2000; Lawrence & Hemmens, 2008; Myers, 2001).

Net widening also occurs due to the effect of policies. For example, Mears and Field (2000) describe a policy in one large urban jurisdiction where the prosecutors automatically sought judicial waiver in all eligible cases. This is not to say that such policies are not legal; that is, allowed. However, it could suggest that some juvenile offenders are being waived simply as a result of policy without regard to their individual situations or needs. Such a policy creates considerable room for net widening (Butts & Mitchell, 2000; Lawrence & Hemmens, 2008; Myers, 2001).

Howell's (1996) review of judicial waiver studies found that on average, 42 percent of waived juveniles were serious property offenders and 47 percent were violent offenders. These findings suggest those judicial waivers generally are reserved for serious offenses. Howell (1996) also found that these percentages varied greatly across jurisdictions. In some, waiver cases consisted primarily of serious and violent offenders, whereas in others, they consisted primarily of less serious offenders. Few studies have systematically examined nonjudicial waiver, among those that have similar patterns and variations have been identified (Bishop et al., 1989; Singer, 1996).

Sentencing

Despite the stated goals in many state statutes to increase punishment, studies of waiver show that a juvenile waived to the adult criminal court can result in less tough punishments: dismissals, plea bargains, diversion programs, and probation (Butts & Mitchell, 2000; Lawrence & Hemmens, 2008; Myers, 2001). However, Howell (1996) stated that "virtually every study has found that serious and violent juvenile offenders receive longer sentences in adult criminal court than in juvenile court" (Howell, 1996, p. 49). Griffin et al. (2011), on the other hand, state that their attempts to answer the question whether convicted juveniles are sanctioned more severely in the adult system are difficult because the various studies have yielded inconsistent results.

Explanations for why juveniles receive the lesser punishment vary and regardless of the reason, existing research suggest that waiver may be effective in producing greater punishment than would occur in juvenile court but only for the most serious juvenile offenders and may result in less severe punishment for less serious offenders.

Brown and Langan (1998) conducted a national study on juveniles waived to the adult criminal court. The study found that juveniles waived had higher rates of incarceration; 63 percent sentenced to prison and 16 percent to jail terms, and the average prison sentences was 9.25 years. Twenty-one percent were given probation.

A study in New Jersey and New York by Fagan (1995) found that processing juveniles in the adult criminal court resulted in higher rates of incarceration; however, not lengthier sentences. Fagan (1995) also found higher rates of rearrest and re-incarceration among juveniles processed in the adult criminal court.

In St. Louis, Kinder, Verneziano, Fichter, and Azuma (1995) found that waived juveniles did not receive greater punishment. The U.S. General

Accounting Office (1995) study of juveniles waived to the adult criminal court found great variability in incarceration rates by state. For example, in Vermont, 33 percent of juveniles convicted of violent crimes, property crimes, and drug crimes in adult criminal court were incarcerated. Minnesota incarcerated nine out of ten of the waived juveniles convicted of those three types of crimes. Pennsylvania, like Minnesota, incarcerated nine out of ten juveniles waived for violent crimes. Pennsylvania only incarcerated one out of ten transferred juveniles for property crimes.

Research indicates that the meaning and use of waiver can vary dramatically among jurisdictions (Feld, 1999; Howell, 1996; Singer, 1996). This variation makes comparison difficult discover as to what if anything occurs to/for the juvenile across jurisdictions. Sanborn (1994) documented that in the three court settings he studied, waiver was viewed by court actors in quite different ways. In the rural and suburban court settings, probation officers played a more prominent role in the waiver process. There also was greater agreement among court actors about the appropriate use of waiver; belief that the waiver was appropriate to remove juveniles who were beyond rehabilitation and threatened the rehabilitation of others. By contrast, court actors in the urban setting viewed the use of the waiver differently from one another. There was much less trust among them, creating a power struggle over how cases were handled. Such variation may dilute the chances that the intended effects of waiving can be achieved. As important, it largely undermines the legitimacy of the waiver by creating a form of "justice by geography" (Feld, 1991, p. 156), where waiving to the adult criminal court depends almost entirely on where a juvenile commits an offense.

Disproportionate Minority Contact

A disproportionate number of minority youth are prosecuted as adults. The latest statistics from the Department of Justice (2009) show that 67 percent of all juvenile defendants in the adult criminal courts are African American. In addition, 77 percent of all juveniles sent to adult prison are minorities; 60 percent African American, 15 percent Hispanic, 1 percent American Indian, and 1 percent Asian. Furthermore, despite minorities using drugs at a lower rate than Caucasian, juveniles charged in adult court for drug-related crimes are disproportionate; 75 percent are African American (National Household Survey on Drug Abuse, 1997). Ninety-five percent of all juveniles sentenced to prison for drug offenses are minorities.

In Cook County, Illinois, Clarke (1996) found a high proportion of the juveniles waived to adult criminal court were minorities; African American and Hispanics made up 94.7 percent of those waived. In New Mexico, Hispanics and American Indians represent 67 percent of judicially waived cases (Houghtalin & Mays, 1991). The high percentage of minorities among waived juveniles may be explained in part by the fact that minorities are disproportionately arrested for serious crimes.

However, in the Fagan et al. (1987) analysis, the effects of race on the judicial waiver decision were found to be indirect.

REFERENCES

Beccaria, C. (1986). *On crimes and punishments* (D. Young, Trans.). Indianapolis, IN: Hackett.

Bilchik, S. (1999). *A study of juvenile transfers to criminal court in Florida.* Washington, DC: U. S. Department of Justice.

Bilchik, S. (1998). A juvenile justice system for the 21st century. *Crime and Delinquency, 44*(12), 89–101.

Bishop, D. (2004). Injustice and irrationality in contemporary youth policy. *Criminology and Public Policy, 345*, 633–644.

Bishop, D. (2000). Juvenile offenders in the adult criminal justice system. In M. Tonry (Ed.), *Crime and justice: A review of research* (pp. 81–167). Chicago, IL: University of Chicago.

Bishop, D. M., & Frazier, C. E. (2000). Consequences of transfer. In J. Fagan & F. E. Zimring (Eds.), *The changing boundaries of juvenile justice: Transfer of adolescents to the criminal court* (pp. 227–276). Chicago, IL: University of Chicago.

Bishop, D., & Frazier, C. (1996). Race effects in juvenile justice decision making: Finding of statewide analysis. *Journal of Criminal Law and Criminology, 86*, 392–414.

Bishop, D., & Frazier, C. (1991). Transfer of juveniles to criminal court: A case study and analysis of prosecutorial waiver. *Notre Dame Journal of Law, Ethics, and Public Policy, 59*, 281–302.

Bishop, D. M., Frazier, C. E., & Henretta, J. C. (1989). Prosecutorial waiver: Case study of a questionable reform. *Crime and Delinquency, 35*, 179–209.

Bishop, D., Lanza-Kaduce, L., & Frazier, C. (1998). Juvenile justice under attack: An analysis of the causes and impact of recent reforms. *University of Florida Journal of Law and Public Policy, 10*, 129–155.

Bishop, D. M., Frazier, C. E., Lanza-Kaduce, L., & Winner, L. (1996). The transfer of juveniles to criminal court: Does it make a difference? *Crime and Delinquency, 42*, 171–191.

Boyce, A. (1994). Choosing the forum: Prosecutorial discretion and Walker v. State. *Arkansas Law Review, 46*, 985–1011.

Brown, J. M., & Langan, P. A. (1998). *State court sentencing of convicted felons, 1994* (Bureau of Justice Statistics No. NCJ-164614). Washington, DC: U. S. Department of Justice.

Burrow, J. (2008). Reverser and the effects of legal statutory and secondary legal factors on sentencing outcomes for juvenile offenders. *Crime and Delinquency, 54*(1), 34–64.

Butts, J. A., & Harrell, A. (1998). *Delinquents or criminals: Policy options for young offenders*. Washington, DC: Urban Institute.

Butts, J. A., & Mitchell, O. (2000). Brick by brick: Dismantling the border between juvenile and adult justice. In C. M. Friel (Ed.), *Boundary changes in criminal justice organizations* (Vol. 22, pp. 167–213). Washington, DC: National Institute of Justice.

Cintron, L. (1996). Rehabilitating the juvenile court system: Juvenile transfers to adult criminal court. *Northwestern University Law Review, 90*, 1254–1280.

Coalition for Juvenile Justice. (2005). *Childhood on trial the failure of trying and sentencing youth in adult criminal court* (Coalition for Juvenile Justice). Washington, DC: U. S. Department of Justice.

Clarke, E. E. (1996). A case for reinventing juvenile transfer. *Juvenile and Family Court Journal, 47*(4), 3–21.

Davis, S. (2000). The criminalization of juvenile justice: Legislative responses to the phantom menace. *Mississippi Law Journal, 70*, 1–33.

DeFrances, C. J., & Strom, K. J. (1997). *Juveniles prosecuted in state criminal courts* (Bureau of Justice Statistics). Washington, DC: U. S. Department of Justice.

Fagan, J. A. (1996). The comparative advantage of juvenile versus criminal court sanctions on recidivism among adolescent felony offenders. *Law and Policy, 18*, 77–113.

Fagan, J. (1995). *Separating the men from the boys: The comparative advantage of juvenile versus criminal court sanctions on recidivism among adolescent felony offenders*. Thousand Oaks, CA: Sage.

Fagan, J., Forst, M., & Vivona, T. S. (1987). Racial determinants of the judicial transfer decision: Prosecuting violent youth in criminal court. *Crime and Delinquency, 33*(2), 259–286.

Feld, B. C. (2004). Editorial introduction: Juvenile transfer. *Criminology and Public Policy, 345*, 599–604.

Feld, B. C. (1999, July 1). The honest politician's guide to juvenile justice in the twenty-first century. *The American Academy of Political and Social Science, 564*, 10–27.

Feld, B. C. (1991). Justice by geography: Urban, suburban, and rural variations in juvenile justice administration. *Journal of Criminal Law and Criminology, 82*, 156–210.

Forst, M., Fagan, J. and Vivona, T.S. (1989), *Youth In Prisons and Training Schools: Perceptions and Consequences of the Treatment-Custody Dichotomy.* Juvenile and Family Court Journal, 40: 1–14. https://doi.org/10.1111/j.1755-6988.1989.tb00634.x

Glassner, B., Ksander, M., Berg, B., & Johnson, B. D. (1983). A note on the deterrent effects of juvenile versus adult jurisdiction. *Social Problems, 31*, 219–221.

Gragg, F. (1986). *Juveniles in adult court: A review of transfers at the habitual serious and violent juvenile offender program sites* (American Institutes for Research). Washington, DC: U. S. Department of Justice.

Griffin, P., Addie, S., Adams, B., & Firestine, K. (2011). *Trying juveniles as adults: An analysis of state transfer laws and reporting* (Office of Juvenile Justice and Delinquency Prevention No. 232434). Washington, DC: U.S. Department of Justice.

Houghtalin, M., & Mays, G. L. (1991). Criminal dispositions of New Mexico juveniles transferred to adult court. *Crime and Delinquency, 37*(349), 393–407.
Howell, J. C. (1996). Juvenile transfers to the criminal justice system: State of the art. *Law and Policy, 18*, 17–60.
Jensen, E., & Metsger, L. (1994). A test of the deterrent effects of legislative waiver on violent juvenile crime. *Crime and Delinquency, 40*, 96–104.
Jeter, H. R. (1922). *The Chicago juvenile court.* Washington, DC: United States Government Printing Office.
Jordan, K. L., & Freibuger, T. L. (2010). Examining the impact of race and ethnicity on the sentencing of juveniles in adult court. *Criminal Justice Policy Review, 21*, 185–201.
Jordan, K. L., & Myers D. L. (2011). Juvenile transfer and deterrence: Reexamining the effectiveness of a "get-tough" policy. *Crime & Delinquency, 57*, 247–270.
Kinder, K., Veneziano, C., Fichter, M., & Azuma, H. (1995). A comparison of the dispositions of juvenile offenders certified as adults with juvenile offenders not certified. *Juvenile and Family Court Journal, 46*, 37–42.
Kurlycheck, M., & Johnson, B. (2004). The juvenile penalty: A comparison of juvenile and young adult sentencing outcomes in criminal court. *Criminology, 42*, 485–517.
Lanza-Kaduce, L., Lane, J., Bishop, D. M., & Frazier, C. E. (2005). Juvenile offenders and adult felony recidivism: The impact of transfer. *Journal of Crime and Justice, 28*, 59–77.
Lawrence, R., & Hemmens, C. (2008). *Juvenile justice a text/reader.* Los Angeles, CA: Sage.
Lee, D. S., & McCrary, J. (2005). *Crime punishment and myopia.* Cambridge, MA: National Bureau of Economic Research.
Macan, H. N., & Rees, D. I. (2005). Economic conditions, deterrence, and juvenile crime: Evidence from micro data. *American Law and Economics Review, 7*, 319–349.
Maitland, A. S., & Sluder, R. D. (1998). Victimization and youthful prison offenders: An empirical analysis. *Prison Journal, 78*, 55–73.
Mason, C. A., & Chang, S. (2001). *Re-arrest rates among youth incarcerated in adult court.* Miami, FL: Miami-Dade County Public Defender's Office.
McShane, M. D., & Williams, F. P. (1989). The prison adjustment of juvenile offenders. *Crime and Delinquency, 35*, 254–269.
Mears, D. P. (2003). A critique of waiver research: Critical next steps in assessing the impacts of laws for transferring juveniles to the criminal justice system. *Youth Violence and Juvenile Justice, 1*, 156–172.
Mears, D. P., & Butts, J. A. (2008). Using performance monitoring to improve the accountability, operations, and effectiveness of juvenile justice. *Criminal Justice Policy Review, 19*, 264–284.
Mears, D. P., & Field, S. H. (2000). Theorizing sanctioning in a criminalized juvenile court. *Criminology, 38*, 983–1020.
McCarthy, F. (1994). The serious juvenile offender and juvenile court reform: The case for prosecutorial waiver of juvenile court jurisdiction. *St. Louis University Law Review, 345*, 629–671.

McCord, J., Widom, K. S., & Crowell, N. A. (2001). Panel of juvenile crime. In *Juvenile Crime, Juvenile Justice.* Washington, DC: National Academy Press.

Myers, D. L. (2005). *Boys among men trying and sentencing juveniles as adults.* Westport, CT: Praeger.

Myers, D. L. (2003). Adult crime, adult time: Punishing violent youth in the adult criminal justice system. *Youth Violence and Juvenile Justice, 18*, 173–197.

Myers, D. L., & Kiehl, K. (2001). The pre-dispositional status of violent youthful offenders: Is there a "custody gap" in adult criminal court? *Justice Research and Policy, 345*(12), 115–143.

National household survey on drug abuse: Population estimates 1997 (DHSS Substance Abuse and Mental Health Services Administration). (1998).

National Research Council Staff (2000). *Juvenile crime, juvenile justice.* Washington, DC: National Academies Press (pp. 154–227).

National Research Council and Institute of Medicine (2001). *Juvenile Crime, Juvenile Justice.* Washington, DC: The National Academies Press. https://doi.org/10.17226/9747.

Podkopacz, M. R., & Feld, B. C. (1996). The end of the line: An empirical study of judicial waiver. *Criminal Law and Criminology, 86*(2), 449–492.

Poulos, T. M., & Orchowsky, S. (1994). Serious juvenile offenders: Predicting the probability of transfer to criminal court. *Crime and Delinquency, 40*(12), 3–17.

Risler, E., Sweatman, T., & Nackerud, L. (1998). Evaluating the Georgia legislative waivers effectiveness in deterring juvenile crime. *Research on Social Work Practices, 86*, 657–667.

Redding, R. E. (2008). *Juvenile transfer laws: An effective deterrent to delinquency?* (Office of Juvenile Justice and Delinquency Prevention). Washington, DC: U. S. Department of Justice.

Redding, R. E., & Fuller, E. J. (2004). What do juvenile offenders know about being tried as adults?: Implications for deterrence. *Juvenile and Family Court Journal, 55*, 35–45.

Sabo, S. (1996). Rights of passage: An analysis of waiver of juvenile court jurisdiction. *Fordham Law Review, 64*, 2425–2454.

Sanborn, J. B. (1994). Certification to criminal court: The important policy questions of how, when, and why. *Crime and Delinquency, 40*, 262–281.

Sanborn, J. B., & Salerno, A. W. (2005). *The juvenile justice system law and process.* Los Angeles, CA: Roxbury.

Schlossman, S. L. (1977). *Love and the American delinquent: The theory and practice of "progressive" juvenile justice.* Chicago, IL: University of Chicago.

Sherman, L. W., & Wisburd, D. (1995). General deterrence effects of police patrol in crime "Hot Spots": A randomized, controlled trial. *Justice Quarterly, 12,* 625–648.

Sickmund, M., Stahl, A. L., Finnegan, T. A., Snyder, H. N., Poole, R. S., & Butts, J. A. (1998). *Juvenile court statistics, 1995* (Office of Juvenile Justice and Delinquency Prevention). Washington, DC: U. S. Department of Justice.

Singer, S. I. (1996). *Recriminalizing delinquency violent juvenile crime and juvenile justice reform.* New York: Cambridge.

Singer, S. I., & McDowall, D. (1988). Criminalizing delinquency: The deterrent effects of the New York juvenile offender law. *Law and Society Review, 22*(349), 521–535.

Smith, D. A., & Gartin, P. R. (1989). Specifying specific deterrence: The influence of arrest on future criminal activity. *American Sociological Review, 54*(1), 34–64, 94–105.

Snyder, H. N., & Sickmund, M. (1999). *Juvenile offenders and victims: 1999 national report.* Washington, DC: U. S. Department of Justice.

Stahl, A. L., Finnegan, T. A., & Kang, W. (2007). *Easy access to juvenile court statistics: 1985–2004*. Pittsburg, PA: National Center for Juvenile Justice.

Stahl, A. L., Finnegan, T. A., & Kang, W. (2002). *Easy access to juvenile court statistics: 1990–1999*. Pittsburg, PA: National Center for Juvenile Justice.

Steiner, B., & Wright, E. (2006). Assessing the relative effects of state direct file waiver laws on violent juvenile crime: Deterrence or irrelevance? *Journal of Criminal Law and Criminology, 96*, 1451–1477.

Thomas, C. W., & Bilchik, S. (1985). Prosecuting juveniles in criminal courts: A legal and empirical analysis. *The Journal of Criminal Law and Criminology, 76*(2), 439–479.

U.S. General Accounting Office. (1995). *Juvenile justice: Juveniles processed in the criminal court and case dispositions* (Tech. Rep. No. GAO/GGD-95-170). Washington, DC: U.S. Government Printing Office.

Winner, L., Lanza-Kaduce, L., Bishop, D. M., & Frazier, C. E. (1997). The transfer of juveniles to criminal court: Reexamining recidivism over the long term. *Crime and Delinquency, 43*, 548–563.

Young, M. C., & Gainsborough, J. (2000). *Prosecuting juveniles in adult court an assessment of trends and consequences*. Washington, DC: The Sentencing Project.

Chapter 6

Effects of Waivers

Peter S. Lehmann and Addison Kobie

Even in the early days of the juvenile court, the option to waive youth offenders to the adult justice system was available to judges, though there were alternative rationales underlying this practice. On one hand, in light of jurisdictional issues that had yet to be clarified, juvenile court officials were reluctant to challenge decisions made by state's attorneys to prosecute the most serious cases in the adult court (Feld, 2019; Myers, 2005; Tanenhaus, 2004). As a result, although states had begun to set clear age limits on juvenile court jurisdiction, transfer to the adult system "served as a built-in safety valve which a judge could use to relieve political pressure on his court by expelling a controversial case" (Tanenhaus, 2000, p. 21). In contrast, judges also sometimes justified the use of transfer as a means of protecting the welfare of children housed in reform schools, which were intended for youth who would most benefit from individualized, lenient, and non-stigmatizing forms of sanctioning (Bishop, 2000; Platt, 1977). Further, there were criticisms of juvenile courts arising in the 1920s and 1930s, which characterized them as soft on crime, and even Progressive supporters of the new juvenile justice system embraced the practice of transfer as essential for the proper functioning of youth courts (Tanenhaus, 2004).

By the 1950s, much of the rhetoric surrounding transfer emphasized the enhanced procedural fairness and the incapacitative and deterrence benefits that processing and punishment by the adult court ostensibly could provide (Bernard & Kurlychek, 2010; Feld, 2019). Indeed, mid-century legal scholars were concerned that the informality and rehabilitative focus of the juvenile court were ineffective at deterring youth crime (e.g., see: Tappan, 1946), and some advocated for a more formalized juvenile court and increased use of waiver, which previously had been a relatively rare and largely symbolic occurrence (Feld, 1999a; Manfredi, 1998). Consequently, as a report by the Advisory Council of Judges of the National Council on Crime and Delinquency (1962) revealed, when justifying transfer decisions, judges frequently considered such factors as the "hopeless" nature of a case, the presumed "advantage in resources for treatment and public safety" offered by the criminal court, and a perceived need to punish a youth especially severely "for his attitude" (p. 5). Then, in a series of landmark decisions during the 1960s and 1970s, the U.S. Supreme Court effectively brought an end to traditional juvenile justice through the imposition of formal procedures and due process protections (Feld, 2003, 2019), thereby ushering in a new era in which "'just deserts' replaced 'justice for the child' as the rallying cry of reformers" (Tanenhaus, 2000, p. 33).

An overtly punitive rationale for transfer became even more prominent during the "get tough" era of the 1980s and 1990s. In response to public fears surrounding a predicted increase in youth crime and the rise of a new class of "juvenile superpredators" (DiIulio, 1995), legislatures enacted a wide range of measures designed to expand the practice of transfer (Bernard & Kurlychek, 2010; Mears, 2002). The first strategy involved expanding modes of transfer beyond discretionary waiver to include prosecutorial direct-file and statutory exclusions, both of which bypass the juvenile court entirely and shift discretion over the transfer decision from juvenile court judges to other criminal justice actors (Bishop, 2000; Feld, 2018; Myers, 2005). Some states also lowered the age of juvenile court exclusion from eighteen years old to fifteen or sixteen (Griffin Addie, Adams, & Firestine, 2011), and others reduced or eliminated entirely the minimum age of transfer (Siennick, 2017). Many scholars expressed concerns that these policy changes reflected a further abandonment of the juvenile court's founding principles and represented a shift in focus from the protection of youths' best interests to retribution, "just deserts," and the protection of public safety (Butts & Mitchell, 2000; Feld, 1999b, 2003; Shook, 2005; Singer, 1997).

As American juvenile justice has transitioned from the "get tough" era to the "kids are different" era (Feld, 2019), much scholarship has explored the legal, ethical, and empirical dimensions of juvenile transfer policy and practice. For instance, a vast body of work from developmental psychology has found striking differences in moral decision-making between youths and adults, with adolescents far less able to thoughtfully consider the consequences of criminal acts (e.g., Cauffman & Steinberg, 2000; Fried & Reppucci, 2001; Steinberg & Cauffman, 1996; Sullivan, 2019). Other research has shown that transfer to the adult court largely fails to provide any specific deterrence benefits (Jordan & Myers, 2011; Redding, 2003; Zane, Welsh, & Mears, 2016), but instead can have a wide range of negative consequences on employment, earning potential, social capital, and the likelihood of recidivism (e.g., Augustyn & Loughran, 2017; Augustyn & McGloin, 2018; Bishop, Frazier,

Lanza-Kaduce, & Winner, 1996; Myers, 2003b; Sharlein, 2018; Taylor, 2015; Winner, Lanza-Kaduce, Bishop, & Frazier, 1997). Further, when examining incarceration experiences, scholars have found that juvenile transfer status is associated with increased institutional misconduct (Haerle, 2019; Kolivoski & Shook, 2016), worsened health outcomes (Valentine, Restivo, & Wright, 2019), and a heightened risk of victimization (Gaarder & Belknap, 2002; Reddington & Sapp, 1997).

While the literature on these issues surrounding transfer has been informative, another broad line of inquiry that also has received much scholarly attention is the punishments that transferred youth receive in the adult court. This latter body of work has provided crucial insights in several areas. First, some of this research has tested the existence of a "juvenile justice model" and a "criminal justice model" of sanctioning in the juvenile and adult courts, respectively (Kupchik, 2003), and some of the reported findings challenge the notion that transfer to the adult court necessarily results in more certain and severe punishment outcomes (Bortner, 1986; Jordan & Myers, 2011; Kupchik, 2006; Myers, 2003a). Second, scholars have explored whether a "juvenile penalty" exists in adult court sentencing, suggesting that there may be attributions connected to culpability and dangerousness that criminal court actors can assign to transferred youth (Johnson & Kurlychek, 2012; Jordan & McNeal, 2016; Kurlychek & Johnson, 2004, 2010). Finally, some research has attempted to explain variability in the sentencing of transferred youth as a unique defendant population, thus investigating the defendant- and contextual-level factors that might inform court actors' perceptions of transferred juveniles and influence the adult court sentencing outcomes that they give to them (Carmichael, 2010; Jordan & Freiburger, 2010; Lehmann, Chiricos, & Bales, 2017; Zane, 2018).

By exploring these interrelated lines of inquiry, this multi-dimensional body of research helps to clarify the ambiguity surrounding how justice system actors understand the meaning of juvenile transfer itself. For instance, it is plausible that, as in the early days of the juvenile court, judges in the contemporary justice system context may consider juvenile transfer status to be largely symbolic, and they reluctantly sentence large numbers of youth transferred to adult court to avoid political conflict and public scrutiny (Bortner, 1986). Alternatively, since "get tough" era juvenile court reforms have effectively "dismantle[d] the legal and procedural border between juvenile justice and criminal justice" (Butts & Mitchell, 2000, p. 178), it may be that court actors do not conceptually distinguish transferred youth from either their retained peers or their adult counterparts. However, it also is possible the retributive ethic of punitive juvenile justice has infiltrated adult court sentencing practices, thus resulting in the characterization of transferred youth as especially dangerous, threatening, and deserving of "adult time" for "adult crime" (Miller & Applegate, 2015; Myers, 2003a). Further, since it is likely that court actors do not perceive transferred youth as a homogenous defendant population, these processes may be conditional upon a variety of other factors that might make court actors more or less likely to view transfer status as signaling increased culpability and threat. Thus, it may be these other variables that ultimately lead justice system personnel to distinguish "our children" from "other people's children" (Feld, 1999b; Lehmann, 2018; Pickett & Chiricos, 2012).

In this chapter, we review three bodies of literature on the punishment of transferred juveniles. First, we assess the state of the research comparing the punishment of youth in the juvenile and adult justice systems, focusing particularly on the notion of separate "models of justice," the promise of increased certainty and severity of punishment that is presumed to be offered by the criminal court, and the possible existence of a "leniency gap" in sanctioning between these two systems. Second, we examine the literature exploring a "juvenile penalty" versus a "youth discount" in adult court sentencing that might be experienced by transfers relative to adult offenders. Then, we review the work on the legal and extralegal factors, which may inform the sentences that transferred youth can receive. Finally, we conclude by highlighting several promising lines of future inquiry.

MODELS OF JUSTICE AND THE VANISHING "LENIENCY GAP"

As states began to expand transfer policies during the "get tough" era, policymakers implicitly made several key assumptions about the distinctions between the juvenile and adult justice systems. These assumptions in large part relate to presumed differences in punishment structures and sanctioning options available to judges in juvenile and adult courts, with the former primarily interested in assigning lenient, restorative, and protective sanctions and the latter better able to mete out severe punishment outcomes to the serious and chronic youth offenders who most deserve them (Singer, 1997; Zimring, 1998). Notably, however, scholars consistently have demonstrated that the "tough on crime" juvenile justice policy shifts during the 1980s and thereafter (e.g., the adoption of offense-based sanctioning guidelines and the loosening of confidentiality protections) may compromise this assumption, ultimately producing a juvenile court system that largely mirrors the functioning of the adult criminal court (Bernard & Kurlychek, 2010; Butts & Mears, 2001; Zimring, 2005). Nonetheless, the logic of transfer follows from the belief that the juvenile and criminal courts are organized under different "models of justice" and that, as a result, the adult system is better equipped to assign certain, swift, and severe sanctions that are theoretically expected to reduce individual youths' likelihood of reoffending as well as juvenile delinquency rates in general.

It has long been assumed that the juvenile and criminal justice systems operate under fundamentally distinct sets of principles, with "juvenile and adult courts . . . representing rehabilitative and punitive orientations, respectively" (Mears & Field, 2000, p. 1009). Thus, the "juvenile justice model" (Kupchik, 2003, 2006) expects that, in general, retained youth will experience the informal, non-adversarial, and flexible processing and sanctioning that are characteristic of the juvenile justice system (Emerson, 1969; Feld, 1997; Krisberg, 2005). Indeed, at the disposition stage, juveniles can expect to receive interventions that are designed to direct youth to individualized treatment-based services, even if judges adhere to formalized guidelines structures when making these decisions (Baglivio, Greenwald, & Russell, 2015; Howell, 2009; Lehmann, Meldrum, & Greenwald, 2020). These priorities in large part reflect the founding principles of the juvenile court itself, which was explicitly intended to ensure that youth receive non-stigmatizing forms of sanctioning that suit the needs of youth (Platt, 1977; Tanenhaus, 2004). Additionally, punishment under the juvenile justice model involves the intentional consideration of youths' extralegal characteristics, including family circumstances, maturity, cognitive development, future welfare and life opportunities, and amenability to specific forms of treatment (Horwitz & Wasserman, 1980). While this enhanced discretion afforded to court actors can result in unwarranted disparities in punishment (e.g., see Bishop, Leiber, & Johnson, 2010; Bridges & Steen, 1998; Engen, Steen, & Bridges, 2002), the primary goal of the juvenile justice model remains the imposition of lenient and individualized sanctions.

The juvenile justice model stands in stark contrast to the criminal justice model, which is expected to guide the sentencing of offenders within the criminal court (Kupchik, 2003, 2006). Theoretical frameworks attempting to explain this model often have emphasized tensions in court actors' decision-making between the goals of "formal rationality" and "substantive rationality" (Savelsberg, 1992; Ulmer, 1997; Ulmer & Kramer, 1996). Formal rationality involves a consideration of the legal factors most relevant for sentencing (e.g., offense type, criminal history, and sentencing guideline recommendations), while substantively rational criteria include the wide range of extralegal factors and practical concerns that court actors also might take into account. Though prior research consistently has revealed that extralegal factors influence criminal sentencing outcomes, it remains the case that "criminal court actors often take into account fewer social and substantive factors than juvenile court actors, instead restricting their evaluations to considerations of offense severity and prior offending history" (Kupchik,

2006, p. 312). Thus, while criminal court judges retain some discretion even under guidelines systems (Johnson, 2005; Kramer & Ulmer, 2002) and priorities and practices can vary across court communities (Hester, 2017; Ulmer, 2019), much of the sentencing process remains formal, adversarial, and directed by the goals of uniformity, proportionality, "just deserts," and the protection of the community.

Given the distinctions between these two models of justice, the practice of transferring youth to the adult court has implications for the prospect of deterrence. Indeed, the rhetoric surrounding the expansion of transfer in the "get tough" era emphasized the potential reduction in delinquency that transfer policies could produce for the juveniles transferred as well as for the entire population of potential youth offenders (Bishop, 2006; Mears, 2003; Redding & Fuller, 2004; Sanborn, 2003). Although a vast body of work has demonstrated that these anticipated specific and general deterrent effects are weak or nonexistent (e.g., Jordan, 2012; Loughran et al., 2010; Myers, 2003b; Singer & McDowall, 1988; Steiner & Wright, 2006; Steiner, Hemmens, & Bell, 2006; Zane et al., 2016; Zimring & Rushin, 2013), an important question that must be addressed concerns whether, compared to the juvenile court, the criminal justice system actually delivers sanctions that are more swift, certain, and severe—key attributes needed for a punishment to deter offending (Jordan & Myers, 2011; Nagin, Cullen, & Jonson, 2009). Of particular interest is the severity of the sentences, as the retributive and incapacitative goals of the criminal justice model, combined with criminal court judges' ability to assign lengthy incarceration terms in adult jails and prisons, might suggest that juvenile transfer indeed can ensure that youth are given "adult time" for "adult crime."

There are several competing theoretical possibilities regarding how transferred youth might be sanctioned relative to their peers retained in the juvenile court. On one hand, it may be the case that transfer laws work as intended and deliver on the promise of assigning sentences harsher than those available for retained youth. Indeed, this possibility would suggest that transfers are subject to punishment under the criminal justice model, while their juvenile court counterparts are sanctioned in light of the juvenile justice model (Kupchik, 2006; Lehmann, Pickett, Ryon, & Kosloski, 2019). A second possibility, however, is that actors in the criminal court make sharp distinctions between transferred juveniles and other defendants, working to ensure that the sentences they give to transfers are comparatively lenient even to what the youth would have received had they been retained (Bortner, 1986; Podkopacz & Feld, 1996). Further, such a pattern also might emerge as a result of the juvenile justice system's growing reliance on more punitive forms of sanctioning (Butts & Mitchell, 2000; Feld, 1999a), which, rather ironically, would indicate that the juvenile court has been "implementing the deterrence model more effectively than the criminal justice system" (Lemmon, Austin, Verrecchia, & Fetzer, 2005, p. 218). Finally, as a consequence of either a shift in juvenile justice toward a criminal justice model or adult court judges' extensions of leniency to transferred youth, it is plausible that few differences might emerge in the punishment of transferred versus retained youth.

The bulk of the evidence from early studies on differences in punishment severity between transferred and retained juveniles pointed to what scholars termed a "leniency gap" (Bortner, 1986; Champion, 1989; Emerson, 1981; Fritsch, Caeti, & Hemmens, 1996; Gillespie & Norman, 1984; Kinder, Veneziano, Fichter, & Azuma, 1995; Podkopacz & Feld, 1996; Royscher & Edelman, 1981; Sagatun, McCollum, & Edwards, 1985). These studies observed that youth who were transferred to the adult court experienced relative leniency compared to similar youth who were retained in the juvenile court, and these advantages were observed in the decision to incarcerate as well as in the length of the period of confinement (Eigen, 1981; Fagan, 1995; Rudman, Hartstone, Fagan, & Moore, 1986). In contrast, though, some of this research reported more nuanced findings, with the leniency gap observed more notably for property offenders than those convicted of person offenses, with the latter subgroup sometimes receiving lengthy sentences in local jail or state prison (Barnes & Franz, 1989; Bishop, Frazier, & Henretta, 1989; Bishop et al., 1996; Fagan, 1990; Lemmon, Sontheimer, & Saylor, 1991; Podkopacz & Feld, 1996; Thomas & Bilchik, 1985). Notably, however, these findings might be misleading, as Fritsch and colleagues (1996) observed that transferred youth tended not to serve their full sentences, thus eliminating any real differences in incarceration lengths between transferred and retained youth (see also Fagan, 1995).

Theoretically, the pattern of evidence pointing to a leniency gap—much of which emerged at the dawn of the "get tough" era—may be explained in several ways. For instance, Bortner's (1986) quantitative and qualitative analysis of court actors' attitudes and perceptions surrounding transfer revealed that despite the traditional rationale of waiver emphasizing deterrence and incapacitation, prosecutors and judges mostly were concerned with confronting political pressures and placating a fearful and punitive public. Indeed, adult court judges typically sentenced transfers to probation or short incarceration terms in light of these defendants' "youthfulness and resulting vulnerability to the harshness of prison life, the lack of facilities and programs oriented toward young offenders, and the overcrowding of the adult system" (Bortner, 1986, p. 57). Another possibility is that adult court judges may have been inclined to sentence transferred youth offenders to community supervision due to their often-limited criminal histories, whereas otherwise similar retained youth were typically housed in secure facilities by the juvenile court (Lemmon et al., 2005). Unfortunately, however, data limitations prevented many researchers from directly assessing what factors might explain sanctioning disparities between the two systems. More importantly, few of these studies provided methodologically rigorous comparisons between samples of transferred and retained youth, and some failed to use multivariate analyses to account for potential confounders (Jordan & Myers, 2011; Myers, 2003a).

In the past two decades, several studies have further explored the disparities in juvenile offender punishment severity between the two systems, and this work generally has provided support for the notion that adult courts assign harsher sanctions. For instance, using data from Pennsylvania, Myers (2003a) found that transferred juveniles were substantially more likely to receive incarceration sentences as well as longer sentences than similar retained youth. Lemmon and colleagues (2005) reported a similar set of findings, observing that the differences in the probability of incarceration remained even after accounting for offense seriousness, juvenile court history, and weapon use. Kupchik's (2006) analysis of data from two states likewise revealed that there indeed is "a punishment tariff to prosecution in criminal court" such that "transfer to criminal court meets its legislatively prescribed goal of punishing adolescents more severely than juvenile courts do" (p. 327). Interestingly, however, in this latter study, no differences emerged in the effects of other legal and extralegal factors on punishment between retained and transferred youth, thus calling into question the existence of distinct juvenile and criminal justice models in the "get tough" era. In a more recent study, Jordan and Myers (2011) observed that, despite mixed effects of transfer status on the likelihood of incarceration, decertified youth (i.e., those remanded back to the juvenile court following waiver) received shorter terms of confinement than youth sentenced in the adult system.

In summary, the bulk of the more recent evidence suggests that, in some sense, juvenile transfer produces its intended effect. Indeed, while the studies by Lemmon et al. (2005) and Jordan and Myers (2011) mentioned earlier found mixed support for the notion that the adult court guarantees other key elements of deterrence, including greater swiftness (i.e., time to disposition) and certainty (i.e., likelihood of conviction), this body of work consistently indicates that the expansion of transfer in the "get tough" era has accomplished its retributive and incapacitative goals. Moreover, this pattern might suggest that justice system actors view the practice in an explicitly punitive light, with transfer status serving as a sign that conveys information about youth's increased blameworthiness, culpability, and risk of recidivism. In fact, recent studies directly assessing the perceptions and behaviors of justice system actors have indicated that prosecutors, judges, and probation officers make notable distinctions between offenders processed in the adult system and those sanctioned by the juvenile court (Bolin & Applegate, 2018; Lehmann et al., 2019). Thus, even as "get tough" juvenile justice policies in many ways have eroded differences in the goals, priorities, and practices between the two systems (Benekos & Merlo, 2008; Kupchik, 2006; Mears, 2002), transfer status in the modern era appears to be a punitive mechanism used to guarantee harsher punishments for the youth who are believed to deserve them.

ASSESSING THE "JUVENILE PENALTY" OR "YOUTH DISCOUNT"

In the eyes of the public, the distinction between youth transferred to the adult court and those retained in the juvenile court is complex. Studies conducted on public attitudes toward youth offenders suggest that, while transfer to the adult court can be a signal of enhanced culpability or dangerousness (Greene, Duke, & Woody, 2017; Semple & Woody, 2011), people generally express substantially more lenient responses to the offending of youth than to that of adults (e.g., Cullen, Fisher, & Applegate, 2000; Mears, Pickett, & Mancini, 2015; Pickett, Welch, Chiricos, & Gertz, 2014; Piquero, Cullen, Unnever, Piquero, & Gordon, 2010; Welch, Butler, & Gertz, 2019). Indeed, while the American public on the whole is in favor of transfer under certain circumstances (Applegate, Davis, & Cullen, 2009; Feiler & Sheley, 1999; Mears, 2001; Miller & Applegate, 2015; Schwartz, Guo, & Kerbs, 1993; Steinberg & Piquero, 2010; Wu, 2000), the public so overwhelmingly supports the notion of "child saving" that optimism surrounding the rehabilitation of youth offenders "can be considered a core cultural belief" (Cullen, Vose, Johnson, & Unnever, 2007, p. 111; see also Mears, Hay, Gertz, & Mancini, 2007; Moon, Sundt, Cullen, & Wright, 2000; Pickett, Chiricos, & Gertz, 2014).

Sympathetic public attitudes toward juvenile offending mirror the findings from a vast body of developmental psychology research, which consistently has demonstrated that "kids are different" (Feld, 2019) by virtue of their reduced cognitive abilities and capacity to properly judge right from wrong (e.g., Cauffman & Steinberg, 2000; Fried & Reppucci, 2001; Grisso & Schwartz, 2000; Steinberg & Cauffman, 1996). As a result, while transfer might be perceived as acceptable in cases that are especially serious or violent, this sanction is commonly viewed as exceptional and to be reserved only for those who are unlikely to be amenable to the rehabilitative influence of juvenile justice system intervention (Miller & Applegate, 2015; Schwartz et al., 1993; Steinberg & Piquero, 2010). Thus, while juvenile lawbreakers in general are viewed as "savable" to an extent that adults are not, transferred youth can be identified as undeserving of special forms of youth court sanctioning and thus are distinguished from "true" juveniles (Mears et al., 2014). Indeed, youth who are transferred often are viewed as unlike those under the care of the juvenile court because their crimes are serious enough that their otherwise limited culpability is no longer in question or the harm done by their offenses is extraordinarily great (Greene et al., 2017; Lehmann et al., 2019). In this way, through the characteristics of their cases or the stigma of transfer itself, youth in the criminal justice system become de facto adults.

Some scholars have argued that, because youth who have been transferred are assigned legal status as adults, it is conceptually inappropriate to equate the adult court sentences that they receive with the interventions given to youth retained in the juvenile court (Kurlychek & Johnson, 2004, 2010; Steiner, 2009). Further, the legal distinction between transferred and retained status reflects dissimilarities in the goals, priorities, and functioning of the two systems. As discussed earlier, even as the juvenile court moved away from its founding principles in recent decades, the two justice systems never became truly identical in these key respects (Butts & Mears, 2001; Feld, 2018; Hay, Ladwig, & Campion, 2018). An important dimension of these differences relates to the characteristics of the sanctions assigned, and prior work clearly has demonstrated that confinement in a juvenile facility is fundamentally dissimilar to an incarceration experience in an adult jail or prison, even for an equal amount of time (Gaarder & Belknap, 2002; Lane, Lanza-Kaduce, Frazier, & Bishop, 2002; Woolard, Odgers, Lanza-Kaduce, & Daglis, 2005). In light of these philosophical and practical distinctions, investigating whether transferred youth are punished more or less harshly than those retained might be less informative than assessing how transfers are sentenced in the adult system relative to adult offenders who are beyond the age of exclusion. Legally and conceptually, these latter defendants arguably more closely represent transferred juveniles' peers.

Several prominent theories of criminal court actors' decision-making can provide insights into how juvenile transfer status might be interpreted by criminal court personnel. For instance, Albonetti's (1991) causal attributions perspective posits that court actors operate in a sentencing context of "bounded rationality" (p. 249) in which limited time, resources, and information about offenders are available. Consequently, as judges attempt to make assessments about defendants' risk of recidivism, they can rely on "patterned responses" that are informed by the extralegal characteristics of the offenders as well as any attendant "stereotypes, prejudices, and highly particularized views" (Clegg & Dunkerley, 1980, p. 265; see also Bridges & Steen, 1998). A similar framework is presented by Steffensmeier, Ulmer, and Kramer (1998), who theorize that sentencing decisions are guided by three broad "focal concerns": blameworthiness, the protection of the community, and the practical constraints and considerations associated with sentencing decisions. As court actors weigh these often-competing priorities in a context characterized by uncertainty and complexity, they can use "perceptual shorthand"

(Steffensmeier et al., 1998, p. 767) or "cognitive heuristics" (Kahneman, 2011) which can involve stereotypes, typescripts, and attributions associated with defendants' membership in various social groups (Farrell & Holmes, 1991; Steffensmeier, Painter-Davis, & Ulmer, 1997). Thus, such factors as an offender's juvenile transfer status might inform sentencing decision-making by providing information that judges use to infer defendants' relative blameworthiness, culpability, dangerousness, or suitability for certain punishments.

While there are strong theoretical reasons to expect that juvenile status could influence judicial actors' perceptions, attitudes, and sentencing decisions, how exactly the unique subpopulation of transferred youth might be understood relative to adults is rather ambiguous. On one hand, it might be reasonable to expect that there could be a "youth discount" (Feld, 2013) such that juvenility acts as a mitigating factor in sentencing. Criminal court actors are likely well aware of developmental differences between juveniles and adults, and the issue of diminished capacity has important implications not only for the legal culpability of youth offenders and the sentences that they deserve (Cauffman & Steinberg, 2000; Kupchik, 2006) but also for any possible deterrence benefits that punitive sentences might confer (Bishop et al., 1996; Jordan, 2012; Loughran et al., 2010; Myers, 2003b). Thus, the especially harsh treatment of youth might be seen by adult court judges as counterproductive and "contrary to the public safety intentions of 'get tough' legislation" (Rainville, 2008, p. 310). Indeed, the potentially harmful effects of lengthy jail or prison terms for youth can be further amplified by a number of practical concerns, including their reduced ability to "do time" in adult facilities (Haerle, 2019; Kolivoski & Shook, 2016) and the long-term negative consequences for youths' educational attainment, employment, and social capital (Augustyn & Loughran, 2017; Augustyn & McGloin, 2018; Sharlein, 2018; Taylor, 2015). Finally, the practice of transfer itself might be viewed as overly punitive, and many court actors may be inclined to sentence juvenile lawbreakers more leniently than adults as a way to correct for legislative and prosecutorial practices that they view as problematic (Kurlychek & Johnson, 2010; Zane, 2018).

In contrast with these possibilities, it may be the case instead that a "juvenile penalty" might emerge in sentencing such that transferred youth are sentenced to harsher outcomes than otherwise similar adult defendants. For instance, given the stigma associated with transfer status, judges might be inclined to view transferred youth defendants as special in ways that make them more threatening to the community. Indeed, rather than entering into the adult court system by default in the same way as offenders beyond the age of exclusion, juvenile transfers may be marked by a unique defendant status that identifies them as "superpredators" (DiIulio, 1995) whose "violent, compunctionless, or incorrigible" (Johnson & Kurlychek, 2012, p. 532) nature distinguishes them as deserving of especially harsh treatment at sentencing. Thus, rather than denoting that the offense at hand was a youthful indiscretion produced by diminished capacity and factors outside the individual's control—key characteristics attributed to delinquency since the early days of the juvenile court (Bernard & Kurlychek, 2010; Platt, 1977), the label of "transferred juvenile" instead might be "an important decision-making cue for identifying the most dangerous, most culpable, or most intractable young offenders" (Kurlychek & Johnson, 2010, p. 731). Consequently, even if criminal court actors support the notion of "child saving" and believe that "kids are different," those sympathies may not extend to transferred youth (Lehmann et al., 2019; Miller & Applegate, 2015).

Perhaps surprisingly, little extant research has assessed whether youth in the adult court are sentenced comparably to older offenders, are extended leniency relative to adults, or are subjected to a "juvenile penalty." Within this body of literature, the bulk of the evidence seems to point to the existence of some kind of "juvenile penalty," though other work has suggested that these effects are likely nuanced. For instance, three studies by Megan Kurlychek and Brian Johnson using data from Pennsylvania and Maryland revealed that transferred youth were more likely to be incarcerated, receive longer sentences, and experience punitive guideline departures than young adults of various ages (Kurlychek & Johnson, 2004, 2010; Johnson & Kurlychek, 2012). Further, in their two more recent studies, these authors made use of matching procedures to limit selection bias that might artificially inflate the effect of juvenile status, but even in their most precise estimates (i.e., between seventeen- and eighteen-year-olds only), the aggravating effect of juvenility on sentencing remained consistent. Steiner (2009) contributed to this line of inquiry by analyzing national data and considering initial detention outcomes in addition to imprisonment, and his study showed that transfers were more likely to be denied bail as well as receive prison sentences than defendants ages eighteen to twenty-nine.

Despite the seemingly clear pattern documented in this research, in several other recent studies more complex patterns have emerged, and these findings have suggested that the juvenile penalty might vary according to the outcome under analysis as well as the adult age group to which youth are compared. For example, Jordan (2014) made use of data from fifty-seven urban counties, and his findings indicated that transferred youth were more likely than older adults to receive sentences to prison, but juveniles were similarly likely to be sentenced to jail as adults of any age group. His analysis of sentence length also revealed mixed findings. In contrast, however, Jordan and McNeal (2016) engaged the same data as Steiner (2009) and observed that, while transferred juveniles received longer jail and prison sentences than adults, juveniles were similarly likely to be imprisoned and were less likely to be sentenced to jail. Complex findings also were reported in a recent study using data from Florida (Lehmann, Chiricos, & Bales, 2018), which found that, while transferred youth were less likely than others to be sentenced to incarceration, the effect of juvenility on sentence length was consistently positive. However, a subsequent study showed that, when these sentencing outcomes were disaggregated, the juvenile penalty most strongly emerged in sentencing to prison (Lehmann, 2018). Finally, one recent study by Kurlychek (2018) using data from New York found that youth ages sixteen and seventeen were consistently sentenced more leniently than others, though these benefits were small relative to those extended to all offenders ages twenty-one and younger as required by state statute.

In short, then, the question of how transferred youth are understood in the criminal court in relation to adult offenders processed by the criminal justice system by default remains unclear. While some evidence indicates that juveniles experience disparately severe punishment outcomes compared to at least some older offenders, other recent studies suggest that this pattern is present in the incarceration decision only, the sentence-length decision only, or neither outcome. Consequently, a key takeaway from this body of research is that juvenile status likely does not carry with it a single meaning in the minds of sentencing judges. Indeed, being a transferred youth defendant is neither a consistent indicator of dangerousness and threat nor clear evidence of immaturity and reduced culpability (Kupchik, 2006; Lehmann et al., 2019). Thus, for scholars to consider all transferred juveniles as belonging to a homogenous defendant subpopulation that criminal court actors evaluate and punish uniformly overlooks the important influence that other legal, extralegal, and contextual factors can have on these perceptions. These additional variables are likely to inform how judges interpret juvenile status, and researchers' exploration of them can help better understand why the "juvenile penalty" might emerge in some circumstances but a "youth discount" can be observed in others.

THE ROLE OF LEGAL AND EXTRALEGAL FACTORS

Transferred juveniles are, on average, far from perfectly comparable to adults, and there are notable distinctions between these two offender subpopulations in several respects. For example, transfers are more likely to be sentenced in the adult court for person offenses than adults (Johnson & Kurlychek, 2012; Kurlychek & Johnson, 2004; Steiner, 2009), and they also tend to have more extensive offending histories as juveniles (Kurlychek & Johnson, 2010). This is not surprising, as transfers do not represent a random subset of youth offenders but rather, on the whole, have cases that are exceptionally serious enough to warrant discretionary waiver or legislative exclusion in the first place. Additionally, simply due to their young age, transferred youth typically have less extensive criminal histories than adults, which is important, given the relevance of criminal history for sentencing outcomes under guidelines systems (Johnson & Kurlychek, 2012; Kurlychek & Johnson, 2010). It is these key differences that have motivated scholars to use matching procedures or other methods to account for selection bias when assessing the "juvenile penalty" versus the "youth discount." However, the legal and extralegal characteristics of cases, as well as the contexts in which criminal courts are situated, are crucial for understanding and explaining variations in the sentencing of transferred youth as a unique defendant subgroup.

The legal attributes of cases generally are the most robust predictors of punishment outcomes for adult criminal defendants, and this remains true for transferred juveniles as well. For instance, McNulty's (1996) analysis of transferred youth sentenced in Arizona found that, in addition to a prior transfer, a violent offense type was the strongest predictor of an incarceration sentence. Other studies of transfers examining data from a wide range of jurisdictions have reported similar findings regarding the prominent role of crime type (Clement, 1997; Houghtalin & Mays, 1991; Jordan & Freiburger, 2010; Rainville, 2008; Steiner, 2005; Zane, 2017). In fact, Kurlychek and Johnson (2004) found that person offenses were sentenced more harshly among transfers than adults, though they later observed a larger "juvenile penalty" among drug cases than violent cases (Kurlychek & Johnson, 2010). Only a few studies have examined the effects of different violent crime types on sentencing outcomes among transfers, and unsurprisingly those convicted of murder receive harsher sentences than those sentenced for rape, robbery, and aggravated assault (Carmichael, 2010; Zane, Singer, & Welsh, 2020). Additionally, while the effects of a juvenile court record and previous arrests are mixed, prior adult criminal convictions and other dimensions of case seriousness consistently produce more severe punishments (Jordan & Freiburger, 2010; Kupchik, 2006; Lehmann et al., 2017; Steiner, 2005, 2009).

While the findings regarding offense type and prior record are informative, scholars generally are more interested in the "substantively rational" dimensions of cases that are outside the domain of the legal factors articulated in statutes and guidelines (Savelsberg, 1992; Ulmer & Kramer, 1996). One such dimension is mode of transfer, and researchers have explored how those who are direct-filed or judicially waived to the adult court are punished relative to youth transferred via statutory exclusion. Theoretically, it is possible that only under some circumstances does transfer symbolize "a prior decision-making juncture in the overall case processing context" (Rainville, 2008, p. 303), and an active exercise of prosecutorial or judicial discretion in particular might "stigmatize the youth as an 'atypical' criminal" (Kurlychek, 2010, p. 7) and signal increased deservingness of punitive treatment. Alternatively, adult court judges may view statutory exclusion laws as representing the political will of the public, and they may believe that the sentencing of these transfers should closely mirror such sentiments (Rainville, 2008; Zane, 2017). The body of work testing these competing theoretical possibilities has produced inconsistent findings, with some research suggesting that those judicially waived are disadvantaged at sentencing (Kurlychek, 2010; Kurlychek & Johnson, 2010; Verrecchia, 2003; Zane, 2017) but others finding a substantial penalty associated with legislative exclusion (Jordan & Freiburger, 2010; Rainville, 2008; Zane et al., 2020). Though these disparate findings might reflect jurisdictional variations in sentencing practices, it is also possible that notable differences between waived and excluded cases were inadequately accounted for, thus producing misleading estimates of the effects of method of transfer (Verrecchia, 2003; Zane, 2017).

Another line of inquiry that scholars have explored is mode of conviction, and some research has found that a conviction at trial can exert direct or interactive effects on the sentencing of transferred youth. Substantial work on adult court sentencing has observed robust evidence of so-called trial penalties, and scholars typically have explained these patterns by pointing to the enhanced negative information about defendants (i.e., "bad facts") that trials can bring to light (Johnson, 2019; Ulmer, 1997; Ulmer & Bradley, 2006). Trials also allow judges greater discretion over the sentencing process, freeing them to rely more heavily on "perceptual shorthand" and "causal attributions" connected to defendants' extralegal characteristics (Johnson, 2003). Given the rare nature of trials, many studies of transferred youth are unable to estimate the effects of mode of conviction (Carmichael, 2010; Jordan & Freiburger, 2010; Kupchik, 2006; Kurlychek, 2010); however, those that do tend to find that juvenile defendants convicted at trial are given harsher sentences than similarly situated transfers who plead guilty (Lehmann et al., 2017; Rainville, 2008; Zane et al., 2020). Additionally, Kurlychek and Johnson (2004) reported that certain trial-plea disparities in sentence severity were larger for juveniles than young adults, but, in contrast, Steiner's (2009) analyses showed larger trial penalties among adults. Lehmann et al. (2018) also observed an interactive relationship between juvenility and mode of conviction, demonstrating that sentencing disparities between adults and juveniles were weaker among trial cases than plea cases.

A key extralegal factor that is theoretically expected to inform the sentencing of transfers is race/ethnicity. The issue of race has been connected to youth sanctioning since the founding of the juvenile court, as judges in the early twentieth century typically intervened only in the lives of poor white youth and immigrants of European ancestry (Bellingham, 1983; Bush, 2010; Platt, 1977). In contrast, black youth were commonly considered to be incorrigible and developmentally stagnant, and for these reasons, the newly defined concepts of "childhood" and "adolescence" were "never extensive enough to include African American children" (Nunn, 2002, p. 679). Thus, as Feld (1999b) has argued, "the Progressive 'child-savers' deliberately designed the juvenile court to discriminate—to 'Americanize' immigrants, to control the poor, and to provide a coercive mechanism to distinguish between 'our children' and 'other people's children' " (p. 339). Although the lobbying efforts of the "black child-savers" in the twentieth century helped to integrate the American juvenile court (Ward, 2012), minority youth since have become overrepresented in juvenile justice institutions (Bishop et al., 2010; Engen et al., 2002; Feld, 1999a). In fact, it has long been argued that the expansion of transfer and other punitive "get tough"–era changes to juvenile justice policy were driven in part by racialized perceptions of juvenile delinquency (Feld, 2003; Jackson & Pabon, 2000; Metcalfe, Pickett, & Mancini, 2015; Pickett & Chiricos, 2012).

Several scholars have explored the ways in which race and ethnicity might affect sentencing outcomes among transferred youth; however, these research findings have been far from conclusive. On one hand, the studies by Jordan and Freiburger (2010) and Howell and Hutto (2012) using the same data from large U.S. counties found rather consistent disadvantages associated with being black on sentence severity, though the effects of Hispanic ethnicity were found to be somewhat less robust. A study from Florida showed a very similar pattern, and black males ages eight to fifteen emerged as a particularly disadvantaged subgroup across several sentencing outcomes (Lehmann et al., 2017). In contrast with these studies, however, McNulty (1996) observed that black and Hispanic transfers in Arizona were not more likely than white youth to receive an incarceration sentence. Other studies likewise found no effects of race or Hispanic ethnicity in Idaho (Steiner, 2005), Pennsylvania (Kurlychek & Johnson, 2004), or New York (Kupchik, 2006). Inconsistent findings were reported based on analyses of national data (Zane, 2017, 2018), though racial/ethnic disparities were found to be rather prominent in pretrial detention. Interestingly, Carmichael's (2010) study showed that, while the direct effects of race/ethnicity were non-significant, black transfers actually received *shorter* sentences than white transfers among murder cases. Finally, though one study found that minority status can amplify juvenile-adult disparities in sentencing (Lehmann, 2018), two others revealed no such pattern (Kurlychek & Johnson, 2004, 2010).

A promising line of inquiry that has received some recent attention relates to the macro-level conditions under which the sentencing of transferred youth can occur. Carmichael (2010) used data collected over a twenty-year period, and he found that a conservative citizen ideology and Republican control of the state government were key for explaining variations in the sentencing of transfers across jurisdictions. In a related study, Carmichael and Burgos (2012) observed that political conservative states as well as those with relatively large black populations handed out more juvenile life sentences—the harshest punishments available for youth offenders. This latter finding regarding macro-level racial/ethnic composition has been explored in depth in a few other studies as well, and some of this work demonstrates that transfers are sentenced especially harshly in counties with large or growing minority populations (Jordan & Maroun, 2016; Zane, 2018). Interestingly, while Steiner (2009) observed an interactive relationship between juvenile status and county-level racial inequality, he found that transferred youth and adults were sentenced more equitably in contexts of heightened racial income inequality.

In conclusion, many advancements in the study of the sentencing of transferred youth have been made in recent years, with scholars providing evidence that a multitude of factors can influence punishment outcomes. Additionally, as highlighted earlier, some research on the "juvenile penalty" has emphasized that this effect is highly conditional, with such variables as offense type, a trial conviction, and minority status amplifying disparities between adults and transferred youth (Kurlychek & Johnson, 2010; Lehmann, 2018; Lehmann et al., 2018). It is clear, then, that to theorize juvenile transfer as having simple and straightforward consequences for sentencing fails to take into account the vast diversity within this special subgroup of criminal cases. Additionally, this work has provided few definitive answers, with the rather inconsistent effects of method of transfer and race/ethnicity in particular sparking much debate. Thus, despite the notable development of this literature in recent years, many key questions surrounding the sentencing of transferred juveniles remain unanswered.

FUTURE DIRECTIONS

From the research on the punishment of transferred youth in the adult criminal court, several broad conclusions can be drawn. First, it appears to be the case that the "leniency gap" observed in the sentencing of transferred versus retained youth during the 1970s and 1980s largely disappeared during the "get tough" era, even though transfer itself has minimal deterrent effects (Jordan & Myers, 2011; Lemmon et al., 2005; Myers, 2003a). Second, while there might be a "juvenile penalty" in the adult court sentencing of transferred youth relative to comparable adult offenders (Kurlychek & Johnson, 2004), this pattern is far from universal across adult comparison groups, sentencing outcomes, or jurisdictional contexts, and under certain circumstances, a "youth discount" can emerge instead (Jordan & McNeal, 2016; Kurlychek,

2018; Lehmann et al., 2018). Finally, as with adult offenders, the factors that inform the sentencing of transfers are largely legal in nature, though disparities in accordance with extralegal factors such as method of transfer, mode of conviction, and race/ethnicity have been observed in a number of studies as well. The empirical literature reviewed earlier is nowhere close to providing clear and consistent answers to the important questions posed by scholars and practitioners, and several lines of inquiry in this area are ripe for further research.

As Feld (2018, 2019) and others have described, the landscape of juvenile court has been undergoing substantial changes in recent years, as courts have begun to scale back their use of transfer and rely instead on various forms of evidence-based juvenile justice (Hay et al., 2018; Sullivan, 2019). In this evolving context, it remains unclear if the patterns observed in the vast body of work reviewed in this chapter will remain consistent or if, instead, the "kids are different" era will be attended by entirely new understandings of how transferred youth should be sentenced. Many of the studies summarized in this chapter—even those which have been published in the past several years—rely heavily on data from 1990s and early 2000s. Thus, it is incumbent on scholars to collect and analyze newly collected data on youth who have been transferred. For instance, it may be the case that the "leniency gap" advantaging transferred juveniles will reemerge or the "youth discount" in sentencing relative to adults will become more prominent. Juvenile justice scholars should be encouraged by the wide range of research questions that are heretofore untested in the modern era.

Beyond the pressing need to collect more recent data on transferred youths' punishment outcomes, little research has been able to follow juvenile offenders from the early stages of case processing through conviction to sentencing. A promising area of research in recent years has involved exploring the effects of "cumulative disadvantage" (Kurlychek & Johnson, 2019) experienced by certain offender subgroups (e.g., racial/ethnic minorities) across multiple criminal justice decision-points (e.g., Kutateladze, Andiloro, Johnson, & Spohn, 2014; Sutton, 2013; Wooldredge, Frank, Goulette, & Travis, 2015). One explicit aim of this latter body of literature is to confront the issue of selection bias, as scholars who assess only a single court outcome can produce inaccurate estimates of the predictors of interest. To our knowledge, no prior work has explored in depth the "life course of criminal cases" (Johnson, 2015) among transferred youth. Instead, researchers often have access only to information on juveniles who already have been transferred, thus precluding a thorough analysis of case processing from arrest to adult court sentencing. Such an approach would provide valuable insights into how transferred youth are perceived by the many different criminal justice actors with whom they come into contact (Lehmann et al., 2019). Qualitative research documenting the experiences of youth as well as the perceptions of court personnel could be especially informative.

A third important line of inquiry warranting further investigation concerns the relationship between race/ethnicity and the sentencing of transferred youth. Given the strong racial undertones of the political rhetoric justifying the expansion of transfer in the 1990s, it is not unexpected that at least some studies show that minority youth are sentenced disparately harshly in the adult court (Jordan & Freiburger, 2010; Lehmann, 2018; Lehmann et al., 2017). However, because the effects of race/ethnicity on the probability of transfer often cannot be accounted for using the data that are commonly available, it is perhaps also unsurprising that this body of work has reported rather inconclusive findings. Additionally, it is unclear the extent to which the practice of transfer will remain conflated with minority status in the "kids are different" era, and further work is needed to uncover whether these patterns have persisted, have been amplified, or have diminished in the past decade. Scholars also should give further consideration to the various offender- and contextual-level factors which might strengthen or mitigate racial and ethnic inequalities in the sentencing of transferred youth.

Finally, there is a clear need to assess the criminal court sentencing consequences of recent changes to juvenile transfer policy. Indeed, not only might the "raise the age" movement and other such reforms have complex effects on rates of juvenile delinquency (Fowler & Kurlychek, 2018; Loeffler & Chalfin, 2017), but these policy shifts also might signal to court actors in those jurisdictions that transferred youth should be perceived as distinct from other juvenile and adult offenders and, as such, must be sentenced under a "juvenile justice model" (Kupchik, 2003). Thus, while more research in this area in general is warranted, a focus on those states and locales that have begun implementing new practices and procedures can be especially enlightening. Indeed, as the practice of juvenile transfer itself continues to evolve, the meaning of youths' transfer status for justice system actors remains dynamic, and researchers must strive to examine and reexamine questions about the punishment of transferred youth.

REFERENCES

Advisory Council of Judges, National Council on Crime and Delinquency. (1962). Transfer of cases between juvenile and criminal courts: A policy statement. *Crime & Delinquency, 8*, 3–11.

Albonetti, C. A. (1991). An integration of theories to explain judicial discretion. *Social Problems, 38*, 247–266.

Applegate, B. K., Davis, R. K., & Cullen, F. T. (2009). Reconsidering child saving: The extent and correlates of public support for excluding youths from the juvenile court. *Crime & Delinquency, 55*, 51–77.

Augustyn, M. B., & Loughran, T. A. (2017). Juvenile waiver as a mechanism of social stratification: A focus on human capital. *Criminology, 55*, 405–437.

Augustyn, M. B., & McGloin, J. M. (2018). Revisiting juvenile waiver: Integrating the incapacitation experience. *Criminology, 56*, 154–190.

Baglivio, M. T., Greenwald, M. A., & Russell, M. (2015). Assessing the implications of a structured decision-making tool for recidivism in a statewide analysis: Disposition matrix for court recommendations made by juvenile probation officers. *Criminology & Public Policy, 14*, 5–49.

Barnes, C. W., & Franz, R. S. (1989). Questionably adult: Determinants and effects of the juvenile waiver decision. *Justice Quarterly, 6*, 117–135.

Bellingham, B. (1983). The "unspeakable blessing": Street children, reform rhetoric, and misery in early industrial capitalism. *Politics & Society, 12*, 303–330.

Benekos, P. J., & Merlo, A. V. (2008). Juvenile justice: The legacy of punitive policy. *Youth Violence and Juvenile Justice, 6*, 28–46.

Bernard, T. J., & Kurlychek, M. C. (2010). *The cycle of juvenile justice*. New York, NY: Oxford University Press.

Bishop, D. M. (2000). Juvenile offenders in the adult criminal justice system. *Crime and Justice, 27*, 81–167.

Bishop, D. M. (2006). Public opinion and juvenile justice policy: Myths and misconceptions. *Criminology & Public Policy, 5*, 653–664.

Bishop, D. M., Frazier, C. E., & Henretta, J. C. (1989). Prosecutorial waiver: Case study of a questionable reform. *Crime & Delinquency, 35*, 179–201.

Bishop, D. M., Frazier, C. E., Lanza-Kaduce, L., & Winner, L. (1996). The transfer of juveniles to criminal court: Does it make a difference? *Crime & Delinquency, 42*, 171–191.

Bishop, D. M., Leiber, M., & Johnson, J. (2010). Contexts of decision making in the juvenile justice system: An organizational approach to understanding minority overrepresentation. *Youth Violence and Juvenile Justice, 8*, 213–233.

Bolin, R. M., & Applegate, B. K. (2018). Supervising juveniles and adults: Organizational context, professional orientations, and probation and parole officer behaviors. *Journal of Crime and Justice, 41*, 410–426.

Bortner, M. A. (1986). Traditional rhetoric, organizational realities: Remand of juveniles to adult court. *Crime & Delinquency, 32*, 53–73.

Bridges, G. S., & Steen, S. (1998). Racial disparities in official assessments of juvenile offenders: Attributional stereotypes as mediating mechanisms. *American Sociological Review, 63*, 554–570.

Bush, W. S. (2010). *Who gets a childhood? Race and juvenile justice in twentieth-century Texas*. Athens, GA: University of Georgia Press.

Butts, J. A., & Mears, D. P. (2001). Reviving juvenile justice in a get-tough era. *Youth & Society, 33*, 169–198.

Butts, J. A., & Mitchell, O. (2000). Brick by brick: Dismantling the border between juvenile and adult justice. *Criminal Justice, 2*, 167–213.

Carmichael, J. T. (2010). Sentencing disparities for juvenile offenders sentenced to adult prisons: An individual and contextual analysis. *Journal of Criminal Justice, 38*, 747–757.

Carmichael, J. T., & Burgos, G. (2012). Sentencing juvenile offenders to life in prison: The political sociology of juvenile punishment. *American Journal of Criminal Justice, 37*, 602–629.

Cauffman, E., & Steinberg, L. (2000). (Im)maturity of judgment in adolescence: Why adolescents may be less culpable than adults. *Behavioral Sciences & the Law, 18*, 741–760.

Champion, D. J. (1989). Teenage felons and waiver hearings: Some recent trends, 1980–1988. *Crime & Delinquency, 35*, 577–585.

Clegg, S., & Dunkerley, D. (1980). *Organization, class and control*. Boston, MA: Routledge and Kegan Paul.

Clement, M. J. (1997). A five-year study of juvenile waiver and adult sentences: Implications for policy. *Criminal Justice Policy Review, 8*, 201–219.

Cullen, F. T., Fisher, B. S., & Applegate, B. K. (2000). Public opinion about punishment and corrections. *Crime and Justice, 27*, 1–79.

Cullen, F. T., Vose, B. A., Jonson, C. N. L., & Unnever, J. D. (2007). Public support for early intervention: Is child saving a "habit of the heart"? *Victims & Offenders, 2*, 109–124.

DiIulio, J. J. (1995). The coming of the super-predators. *The Weekly Standard, 1*, 23–28.

Eigen, J. P. (1981). Punishing youth homicide offenders in Philadelphia. *Journal of Criminal Law & Criminology, 72*, 1072–1093.

Emerson, R. M. (1969). *Judging delinquents: Contexts and process in juvenile court*. Piscataway, NJ: Transaction Publishers.

Emerson, R. M. (1981). On last resorts. *American Journal of Sociology, 87*, 1–22.

Engen, R. L., Steen, S., & Bridges, G. S. (2002). Racial disparities in the punishment of youth: A theoretical and empirical assessment of the literature. *Social Problems, 49*, 194–220.

Fagan, J. (1990). Social and legal policy dimensions of violent juvenile crime. *Criminal Justice and Behavior, 17*, 93–133.

Fagan, J. (1995). Separating the men from the boys: The comparative advantage of juvenile versus criminal court sanctions on recidivism among adolescent felony offenders. In J. C. Howell, B. Krisberg, J. D. Hawkins, & J. J. Wilson (Eds.), *A sourcebook: Serious, violent, & chronic juvenile offenders* (pp. 238–260). Thousand Oaks, CA: Sage.

Farrell, R. A., & Holmes, M. D. (1991). The social and cognitive structure of legal decision-making. *The Sociological Quarterly, 32*, 529–542.

Feiler, S., & Sheley, J. (1999). Legal and racial elements of public willingness to transfer juvenile offenders to adult court. *Journal of Criminal Justice, 27*, 55–64.

Feld, B. C. (1997). Abolish the juvenile court: Youthfulness, criminal responsibility, and sentencing policy. *Journal of Criminal Law & Criminology, 88*, 68–136.

Feld, B. C. (1999a). *Bad kids: Race and the transformation of the juvenile court*. New York, NY: Oxford University Press.

Feld, B. C. (1999b). The transformation of the juvenile court—part II: Race and the "crack down" on youth crime. *Minnesota Law Review, 84*, 327–395.

Feld, B. C. (2003). The politics of race and juvenile justice: The "due process revolution" and the conservative reaction. *Justice Quarterly, 20*, 765–800.

Feld, B. C. (2013). The youth discount: Old enough to do the crime, too young to do the time. *Ohio State Journal of Criminal Law, 11*, 107–148.

Feld, B. C. (2018). Punishing kids in juvenile and criminal courts. *Crime and Justice, 47*, 417–474.

Feld, B. C. (2019). *The evolution of the juvenile court: Race, politics, and the criminalizing of juvenile justice*. New York, NY: New York University Press.

Fowler, E., & Kurlychek, M. C. (2018). Drawing the line: Empirical recidivism results from a natural experiment raising the age of criminal responsibility. *Youth Violence and Juvenile Justice, 16*, 263–278.

Fried, C. S., & Reppucci, N. D. (2001). Criminal decision making: The development of adolescent judgment, criminal responsibility, and culpability. *Law and Human Behavior, 25*, 45–61.

Fritsch, E. J., Caeti, T. J., & Hemmens, C. (1996). Spare the needle but not the punishment: The incarceration of waived youth in Texas prisons. *Crime & Delinquency, 42*, 593–609.

Gaarder, E., & Belknap, J. (2002). Tenuous borders: Girls transferred to adult court. *Criminology, 40*, 481–517.

Gillespie, L. K., & Norman, M. D. (1984). Does certification mean prison: Some preliminary findings from Utah. *Juvenile & Family Court Journal, 35*, 23–34.

Greene, E., Duke, L., & Woody, W. D. (2017). Stereotypes influence beliefs about transfer and sentencing of juvenile offenders. *Psychology, Crime & Law, 23*, 841–858.

Griffin, P., Addie, S., Adams, B., & Firestine, K. (2011). *Trying juveniles as adults: An analysis of state transfer laws and reporting*. Washington, DC: U.S. Department of Justice, Office of Juvenile Justice and Delinquency Prevention.

Grisso, T. E., & Schwartz, R. G. (Eds.). (2000). *Youth on trial: A developmental perspective on juvenile justice*. Chicago, IL: The University of Chicago Press.

Haerle, D. R. (2019). Unpacking adultification: Institutional experiences and misconduct of adult court and juvenile court youth living under the same roof. *International Journal of Offender Therapy and Comparative Criminology, 63*, 663–693.

Hay, C., Ladwig, S., & Campion, B. (2018). Tracing the rise of evidence-based juvenile justice in Florida. *Victims & Offenders, 13*, 312–335.

Hester, R. (2017). Judicial rotation as centripetal force: Sentencing in the court communities of South Carolina. *Criminology, 55*, 205–235.

Horwitz, A., & Wasserman, M. (1980). Some misleading conceptions in sentencing research: An example and a reformulation in the juvenile court. *Criminology, 18*, 411–424.

Houghtalin, M., & Mays, G. L. (1991). Criminal dispositions of New Mexico juveniles transferred to adult court. *Crime & Delinquency, 37*, 393–407.

Howell, J. C. (2009). *Preventing and reducing juvenile delinquency: A comprehensive framework* (2nd ed.). Thousand Oaks, CA: Sage.

Howell, R. J., & Hutto, T. S. (2012). Sentencing convicted juvenile felony offenders in the adult court: The direct effects of race. *Behavioral Sciences & the Law, 30*, 782–799.

Jackson, R., & Pabon, E. (2000). Race and treating other people's children as adults. *Journal of Criminal Justice, 28*, 507–515.

Johnson, B. D. (2003). Racial and ethnic disparities in sentencing departures across modes of conviction. *Criminology, 41*, 449–490.

Johnson, B. D. (2005). Contextual disparities in guidelines departures: Courtroom social contexts, guidelines compliance, and extralegal disparities in criminal sentencing. *Criminology, 43*, 761–796.

Johnson, B. D. (2015). Examining the life course of criminal cases. *Criminology & Public Policy, 14*, 183–186.

Johnson, B. D. (2019). Trials and tribulations: The trial tax and the process of punishment. *Crime and Justice, 48*, 313–363.

Johnson, B. D., & Kurlychek, M. C. (2012). Transferred juveniles in the era of sentencing guidelines: Examining judicial departures for juvenile offenders in adult criminal court. *Criminology, 50*, 525–564.

Jordan, K. L. (2012). Juvenile transfer and recidivism: A propensity score matching approach. *Journal of Crime and Justice, 35*, 53–67.

Jordan, K. L. (2014). Juvenile status and criminal sentencing: Does it matter in the adult system? *Youth Violence and Juvenile Justice, 12*, 315–331.

Jordan, K. L., & Freiburger, T. L. (2010). Examining the impact of race and ethnicity on the sentencing of juveniles in the adult court. *Criminal Justice Policy Review, 21*, 185–201.

Jordan, K. L., & Maroun, R. (2016). Minority threat and criminal sentencing: Examining juveniles in the adult criminal justice system. *Journal of Crime and Justice, 39*, 41–54.

Jordan, K. L., & McNeal, B. A. (2016). Juvenile penalty or leniency: Sentencing of juveniles in the criminal justice system. *Law and Human Behavior, 40*, 387–400.

Jordan, K. L., & Myers, D. L. (2011). Juvenile transfer and deterrence: Reexamining the effectiveness of a "get-tough" policy. *Crime & Delinquency, 57*, 247–270.

Kahneman, D. (2011). *Thinking, fast and slow.* New York, NY: Farrar, Straus, and Giroux.

Kinder, K., Veneziano, C., Fichter, M., & Azuma, H. (1995). A comparison of the dispositions of juvenile offenders certified as adults with juvenile offenders not certified. *Juvenile and Family Court Journal, 46*, 37–42.

Kolivoski, K. M., & Shook, J. J. (2016). Incarcerating juveniles in adult prisons: Examining the relationship between age and prison behavior in transferred juveniles. *Criminal Justice and Behavior, 43*, 1242–1259.

Kramer, J. H., & Ulmer, J. T. (2002). Downward departures for serious violent offenders: Local court "corrections" to Pennsylvania's sentencing guidelines. *Criminology, 40*, 897–932.

Krisberg, B. (2005). *Juvenile justice: Redeeming our children.* Thousand Oaks, CA: Sage.

Kupchik, A. (2003). Prosecuting adolescents in criminal courts: Criminal or juvenile justice? *Social Problems, 50*, 439–460.
Kupchik, A. (2006). The decision to incarcerate in juvenile and criminal courts. *Criminal Justice Review, 31*, 309–336.
Kurlychek, M. C. (2010). Pathways to adult court: Does the road traveled impact the final destination? *Justice Research and Policy, 12*, 1–24.
Kurlychek, M. C. (2018). Mitigation for minors: Exploring the nuances of social constructs and legal status in structuring sentences for youthful offenders. *Punishment & Society, 20*, 498–522.
Kurlychek, M. C., & Johnson, B. D. (2004). The juvenile penalty: A comparison of juvenile and young adult sentencing outcomes in adult criminal court. *Criminology, 42*, 485–517.
Kurlychek, M. C., & Johnson, B. D. (2010). Juvenility and punishment: Sentencing juveniles in adult criminal court. *Criminology, 48*, 725–758.
Kurlychek, M. C., & Johnson, B. D. (2019). Cumulative disadvantage in the American criminal justice system. *Annual Review of Criminology, 2*, 291–319.
Kutateladze, B. L., Andiloro, N. R., Johnson, B. D., & Spohn, C. C. (2014). Cumulative disadvantage: Examining racial and ethnic disparity in prosecution and sentencing. *Criminology, 52*, 514–551.
Lane, J., Lanza-Kaduce, L., Frazier, C. E., & Bishop, D. M. (2002). Adult versus juvenile sanctions: Voices of incarcerated youths. *Crime & Delinquency, 48*, 431–455.
Lehmann, P. S. (2018). Sentencing other people's children: The intersection of race, gender, and juvenility in the adult criminal court. *Journal of Crime and Justice, 41*, 553–572.
Lehmann, P. S., Chiricos, T., & Bales, W. D. (2017). Sentencing transferred juveniles in the adult criminal court: The direct and interactive effects of race and ethnicity. *Youth Violence and Juvenile Justice, 15*, 172–190.
Lehmann, P. S., Chiricos, T., & Bales, W. D. (2018). Juveniles on trial: Mode of conviction and the adult court sentencing of transferred juveniles. *Crime & Delinquency, 64*, 563–586.
Lehmann, P. S., Meldrum, R. C., & Greenwald, M. A. (2020). Upward departures from structured recommendations in juvenile court dispositions: The intersection of race, ethnicity, and gender. *Justice Quarterly, 37*, 514–540.
Lehmann, P. S., Pickett, J. T., Ryon, S. B., & Kosloski, A. E. (2019). Race, juvenile transfer, and sentencing preferences: Findings from a randomized experiment. *Race and Justice, 9*, 251–275.
Lemmon, J. H., Austin, T. L., Verrecchia, P. J., & Fetzer, M. (2005). The effect of legal and extralegal factors on statutory exclusion of juvenile offenders. *Youth Violence and Juvenile Justice, 3*, 214–234.
Lemmon, J. H., Sontheimer, H., & Saylor, K. A. (1991). *A study of Pennsylvania juveniles transferred to criminal court in 1986*. Harrisburg, PA: Pennsylvania Juvenile Court Judges' Commission.
Loeffler, C. E., & Chalfin, A. (2017). Estimating the crime effects of raising the age of majority. *Criminology & Public Policy, 16*, 45–71.

Loughran, T. A., Mulvey, E. P., Schubert, C. A., Chassin, L. A., Steinberg, L., Piquero, A. R., Fagan, J., Cota-Robles, S., Cauffman, E., & Losoya, S. (2010). Differential effects of adult court transfer on juvenile offender recidivism. *Law and Human Behavior, 34*, 476–488.

Manfredi, C. P. (1998). *The Supreme Court and juvenile justice*. Lawrence, KS: The University Press of Kansas.

McNulty, E. W. (1996). The transfer of juvenile offenders to adult court: Panacea or problem? *Law & Policy, 18*, 61–75.

Mears, D. P. (2001). Getting tough with juvenile offenders: Explaining support for sanctioning youths as adults. *Criminal Justice and Behavior, 28*, 206–226.

Mears, D. P. (2002). Sentencing guidelines and the transformation of juvenile justice in the 21st century. *Journal of Contemporary Criminal Justice, 18*, 6–19.

Mears, D. P. (2003). A critique of waiver research: Critical next steps in assessing the impacts of laws for transferring juveniles to the criminal justice system. *Youth Violence and Juvenile Justice, 1*, 156–172.

Mears, D. P., & Field, S. H. (2000). Theorizing sanctioning in a criminalized juvenile court. *Criminology, 38*, 983–1020.

Mears, D. P., Cochran, J. C., Stults, B. J., Greenman, S. J., Bhati, A. S., & Greenwald, M. A. (2014). The "true" juvenile offender: Age effects and juvenile court sanctioning. *Criminology, 52*, 169–194.

Mears, D. P., Hay, C., Gertz, M., & Mancini, C. (2007). Public opinion and the foundation of the juvenile court. *Criminology, 45*, 223–257.

Mears, D. P., Pickett, J. T., & Mancini, C. (2015). Support for balanced juvenile justice: Assessing views about youth, rehabilitation, and punishment. *Journal of Quantitative Criminology, 31*, 459–479.

Metcalfe, C., Pickett, J. T., & Mancini, C. (2015). Using path analysis to explain racialized support for punitive delinquency policies. *Journal of Quantitative Criminology, 31*, 699–725.

Miller, R. N., & Applegate, B. K. (2015). Adult crime, adult time? Benchmarking public views on punishing serious juvenile felons. *Criminal Justice Review, 40*, 151–168.

Moon, M. M., Sundt, J. L., Cullen, F. T., & Wright, J. P. (2000). Is child saving dead? Public support for juvenile rehabilitation. *Crime & Delinquency, 46*, 38–60.

Myers, D. L. (2003a). Adult crime, adult time: Punishing violent youth in the adult criminal justice system. *Youth Violence and Juvenile Justice, 1*, 173–197.

Myers, D. L. (2003b). The recidivism of violent youths in juvenile and adult court: A consideration of selection bias. *Youth Violence and Juvenile Justice, 1*, 79–101.

Myers, D. L. (2005). *Boys among men: Trying and sentencing juveniles as adults*. Westport, CT: Praeger.

Nagin, D. S., Cullen, F. T., & Jonson, C. L. (2009). Imprisonment and reoffending. *Crime and Justice, 38*, 115–200.

Nunn, K. B. (2002). The child as other: Race and differential treatment in the juvenile justice system. *DePaul Law Review, 51*, 679–714.

Pickett, J. T., & Chiricos, T. (2012). Controlling other people's children: Racialized views of delinquency and White's punitive attitudes toward juvenile offenders. *Criminology, 50*, 673–710.

Pickett, J. T., Chiricos, T., & Gertz, M. (2014). The racial foundations of whites' support for child saving. *Social Science Research, 44*, 44–59.
Pickett, J. T., Welch, K., Chiricos, T., & Gertz, M. (2014). Racial crime stereotypes and offender juvenility: Comparing public views about youth-specific and nonyouth-specific sanctions. *Race and Justice, 4*, 381–405.
Piquero, A. R., Cullen, F. T., Unnever, J. D., Piquero, N. L., & Gordon, J. A. (2010). Never too late: Public optimism about juvenile rehabilitation. *Punishment & Society, 12*, 187–207.
Platt, A. M. (1977). *The child savers: The invention of delinquency*. Chicago, IL: The University of Chicago Press.
Podkopacz, M. R., & Feld, B. C. (1996). End of the line: An empirical study of judicial waiver. *Journal of Criminal Law & Criminology, 86*, 449–492.
Rainville, G. (2008). Juveniles transferred to criminal courts: Is their criminal sentence dependent on how they got there? *Criminal Justice Policy Review, 19*, 301–313.
Redding, R. E. (2003). The effects of adjudicating and sentencing juveniles as adults: Research and policy implications. *Youth Violence and Juvenile Justice, 1*, 128–155.
Redding, R. E., & Fuller, E. J. (2004). What do juvenile offenders know about being tried as adults? Implications for deterrence. *Juvenile and Family Court Journal, 55*, 35–44.
Reddington, F. P., & Sapp, A. D. (1997). Juveniles in adult prisons: Problems and prospects. *Journal of Crime and Justice, 20*, 139–152.
Royscher, M., & Edelman, P. (1981). Treating juveniles as adults in New York: What does it mean and how is it working? In J. C. Hall, D. M. Hamparian, J. M. Pettibone, & J. L. White (Eds.), *Major issues in juvenile justice information and training: Readings in public policy* (pp. 265–293). Columbus, OH: Academy for Contemporary Problems.
Rudman, C., Hartstone, E., Fagan, J., & Moore, M. (1986). Violent youth in adult court: Process and punishment. *Crime & Delinquency, 32*, 75–96.
Sagatun, I., McCollum, L. L., & Edwards, L. P. (1985). The effect of transfers from juvenile to criminal court: A loglinear analysis. *Journal of Crime and Justice, 8*, 65–92.
Sanborn, J. B. (2003). Hard choices or obvious ones: Developing policy for excluding youth from juvenile court. *Youth Violence and Juvenile Justice, 1*, 198–214.
Savelsberg, J. J. (1992). Law that does not fit society: Sentencing guidelines as a neoclassical reaction to the dilemmas of substantivized law. *American Journal of Sociology, 97*, 1346–1381.
Schwartz, I. M., Guo, S., & Kerbs, J. J. (1993). The impact of demographic variables on public opinion regarding juvenile justice: Implications for public policy. *Crime & Delinquency, 39*, 5–28.
Semple, J. K., & Woody, W. D. (2011). Juveniles tried as adults: The age of the juvenile matters. *Psychological Reports, 109*, 301–308.
Sharlein, J. (2018). Beyond recidivism: Investigating comparative educational and employment outcomes for adolescents in the juvenile and criminal justice systems. *Crime & Delinquency, 64*, 26–52.

Shook, J. J. (2005). Contesting childhood in the U.S. justice system: The transfer of juveniles to adult criminal court. *Childhood, 12*, 461–478.

Siennick, S. E. (2017). Drawing, and redrawing, the line between juvenile and adult court jurisdiction. *Criminology & Public Policy, 16*, 41–44.

Singer, S. I. (1997). *Recriminalizing delinquency: Violent juvenile crime and juvenile justice reform*. New York, NY: Cambridge University Press.

Singer, S. I., & McDowall, D. (1988). Criminalizing delinquency: The deterrent effects of the New York juvenile offender law. *Law & Society Review, 22*, 521–535.

Steffensmeier, D., Painter-Davis, N., & Ulmer, J. (2017). Intersectionality of race, ethnicity, gender, and age on criminal punishment. *Sociological Perspectives, 60*, 810–833.

Steffensmeier, D., Ulmer, J., & Kramer, J. (1998). The interaction of race, gender, and age in criminal sentencing: The punishment cost of being young, black, and male. *Criminology, 36*, 763–798.

Steinberg, L., & Cauffman, E. (1996). Maturity of judgment in adolescence: Psychosocial factors in adolescent decision making. *Law and Human Behavior, 20*, 249–272.

Steinberg, L., & Piquero, A. R. (2010). Manipulating public opinion about trying juveniles as adults: An experimental study. *Crime & Delinquency, 56*, 487–506.

Steiner, B. (2005). Predicting sentencing outcomes and time served for juveniles transferred to criminal court in a rural northwestern state. *Journal of Criminal Justice, 33*, 601–610.

Steiner, B. (2009). The effects of juvenile transfer to criminal court on incarceration decisions. *Justice Quarterly, 26*, 77–106.

Steiner, B., & Wright, E. (2006). Assessing the relative effects of state direct file waiver laws on violent juvenile crime: Deterrence or irrelevance? *Journal of Criminal Law & Criminology, 96*, 1451–1477.

Steiner, B., Hemmens, C., & Bell, V. (2006). Legislative waiver reconsidered: General deterrent effects of statutory exclusion laws enacted post-1979. *Justice Quarterly, 23*, 34–59.

Sullivan, C. J. (2019). *Taking juvenile justice seriously: Developmental insights and system challenges*. Philadelphia, PA: Temple University Press.

Sutton, J. R. (2013). Structural bias in the sentencing of felony defendants. *Social Science Research, 42*, 1207–1221.

Tanenhaus, D. S. (2000). The evolution of transfer out of the juvenile court. In J. Fagan & F. E. Zimring (Eds.), *The changing borders of juvenile justice: Transfer of adolescents to the criminal court* (pp. 13–43). Chicago, IL: The University of Chicago Press.

Tanenhaus, D. S. (2004). *Juvenile justice in the making*. New York, NY: Oxford University Press.

Tappan, P. W. (1946). Treatment without trial. *Social Forces, 24*, 306–311.

Taylor, M. (2015). Juvenile transfers to adult court: An examination of the long-term outcomes of transferred and non-transferred juveniles. *Juvenile and Family Court Journal, 66*, 29–47.

Thomas, C. W., & Bilchik, S. (1985). Prosecuting juveniles in criminal courts: A legal and empirical analysis. *Journal of Criminal Law & Criminology, 76*, 439–479.

Ulmer, J. T. (1997). *Social worlds of sentencing: Court communities under sentencing guidelines*. Albany, NY: State University of New York Press.

Ulmer, J. T. (2019). Criminal courts as inhabited institutions: Making sense of difference and similarity in sentencing. *Crime and Justice, 48*, 483–522.

Ulmer, J. T., & Bradley, M. S. (2006). Variation in trial penalties among serious violent offenses. *Criminology, 44*, 631–670.

Ulmer, J. T., & Kramer, J. H. (1996). Court communities under sentencing guidelines: Dilemmas of formal rationality and sentencing disparity. *Criminology, 34*, 383–408.

Valentine, C. L., Restivo, E., & Wright, K. (2019). Prolonged isolation as a predictor of mental health for waived juveniles. *Journal of Offender Rehabilitation, 58*, 352–369.

Verrecchia, P. J. (2003). The effect of transfer mechanism from juvenile court on the likelihood of incarceration in criminal court. *Free Inquiry in Creative Sociology, 31*, 15–23.

Ward, G. (2012). *The black child-savers: Racial democracy and juvenile justice.* Chicago, IL: The University of Chicago Press.

Welch, K., Butler, L. F., & Gertz, M. (2019). Saving children, damning adults? An examination of public support for juvenile rehabilitation and adult punishment. *Criminal Justice Review, 44*, 470–491.

Winner, L., Lanza-Kaduce, L., Bishop, D. M., & Frazier, C. E. (1997). The transfer of juveniles to criminal court: Reexamining recidivism over the long term. *Crime & Delinquency, 43*, 548–563.

Woolard, J. L., Odgers, C., Lanza-Kaduce, L., & Daglis, H. (2005). Juveniles within adult correctional settings: Legal pathways and developmental considerations. *International Journal of Forensic Mental Health, 4*, 1–18.

Wooldredge, J., Frank, J., Goulette, N., & Travis III, L. (2015). Is the impact of cumulative disadvantage on sentencing greater for Black defendants? *Criminology & Public Policy, 14*, 187–223.

Wu, B. (2000). Determinants of public opinion toward juvenile waiver decisions. *Juvenile and Family Court Journal, 51*, 9–20.

Zane, S. N. (2017). Do criminal court outcomes vary by juvenile transfer mechanism? A multi-jurisdictional, multilevel analysis. *Justice Quarterly, 34*, 542–569.

Zane, S. N. (2018). Exploring the minority threat hypothesis for juveniles in criminal court: Static versus dynamic threat and diffuse versus targeted effects. *Youth Violence and Juvenile Justice, 16*, 418–441.

Zane, S. N., Singer, S. I., & Welsh, B. C. (2020). The right to a good defense: Investigating the influence of attorney type across urban counties for juveniles in criminal court. *Criminal Justice Policy Review*. Advance online publication. doi:10.1177/0887403420903376

Zane, S. N., Welsh, B. C., & Mears, D. P. (2016). Juvenile transfer and the specific deterrence hypothesis. *Criminology & Public Policy, 15*, 901–925.

Zimring, F. E. (1998). *American youth violence*. New York, NY: Oxford University Press.
Zimring, F. E. (2005). *American juvenile justice*. New York, NY: Oxford University Press.
Zimring, F. E., & Rushin, S. (2013). Did changes in juvenile sanctions reduce juvenile crime rates; A natural experiment. *Ohio State Journal of Criminal Law, 11*, 57–70.

Conclusion

The Future of Juvenile Transfer

Sheri Jenkins Keenan

The nationwide push toward transferring juveniles to the adult criminal court assumes that more punitive, adult criminal sanctions will act as a deterrent to juvenile crime. Research is mixed on the deterrent effect of transferring juveniles to the adult criminal court.

First, research looking at specific deterrence and juvenile transfers found higher recidivism rates among juveniles convicted for violence offenses in adult criminal court when compared with similar offenders tried in juvenile court. For example, an study by Jensen and Metsger's (1994) in Idaho found a 13 percent increase in arrest rate for violent crime. Other research has found no deterrent effect. For example, a research by Singer and McDowall (1988) in New York and Philadelphia found no deterrent effect on violence juvenile crime, and Lee and McCrary (2005) in their Florida study found that young people did not lower their offending rates suggesting that the prospect of adult sanctions was not a deterrent.

The studies on general deterrence are less clear. The studies have produced somewhat conflicting findings; however, most of the research suggests that transfer laws have little or no general deterrent effect.

The future of juvenile transfer is closely tied to the fate of the juvenile justice system itself, the reauthorization of the Juvenile Justice and Delinquency Prevention Act (JJDPA), and growing acceptance of Adverse Childhood Experiences (ACEs) and trauma-informed approaches to dealing with children and youth.

Public support for a separate juvenile system has declined in the latter part of the twentieth century.

THE JUVENILE JUSTICE SYSTEM

Critics of the juvenile justice system argued that it should be abolished. They claim juvenile courts coddled youthful offenders and rehabilitation was ineffective in many individuals. Furthermore, they claim the juvenile courts were established to handle status offenses such as truancy, not the violent mass murders of the late twentieth century. Finally, they argue that if juvenile offenders believed juvenile courts would hold them fully responsible for their crimes, they would be less likely to commit serious crimes.

Defenders of juvenile justice system argue that juvenile crime rates have decreased, and the court system should not be judged on the highly publicized violent acts of a few. They argue that the court system allows judges to transfer the most violent offenders to adult criminal courts, which did occur on an increasing basis by the early 2000s. Furthermore, they argue that since children and youth are treated differently than adults in every other part of society, it should be the same in the criminal justice system as well.

JUVENILE JUSTICE AND DELINQUENCY PREVENTION ACT

Established in 1974, the JJDPA is based on a consensus that child, youth, and families involved with the criminal justice system should be guarded by federal standards for care and custody while also upholding the interest of community safety and the prevention of victimization. The JJDPA has been reauthorized twice since 1974; 2002 and 2018. The JJDPA sets four core protections with which states must comply to be eligible to receive federal funding under the act. The purpose of each core protection is to safeguard children and youth who encounter the juvenile justice system and to ensure appropriate, safe, and rehabilitative treatment. The four-core protection are: deinstitutionalization of status offenders, sight and sound separation, jail removal, and Racial and Ethnic Disparities.

Under the deinstitutionalization of status offender's protection, children and youth charged with a status offense may not be held in secure detention or confinement. This provision helps to ensure that children and youth who have not committed a delinquent/criminal act are not incarcerated. Under the sight and sound separation protection, when children and youth are placed in an adult jail or lock-up, sight and sound contact with adult inmates is prohibited; children and youth cannot be housed next to adult cells; share dining halls, recreation areas, or common space; or have verbal or nonverbal communication with adult inmates. This protection along with the jail removal protection seeks to protect children and youth from threats, intimidation, and other forms of psychological abuse and physical assault. Research shows that children and youth placed in jails are especially vulnerable to sexual and physical assault and are thirty-six times more likely to commit suicide in jails than in juvenile specific facilities.

ADVERSE CHILDHOOD EXPERIENCES

ACEs have a tremendous impact on future violence victimization, perpetration, and negative effect on lifelong health and economic opportunities. The original ACEs study was conducted by the CDC (Center for Disease Control) and Kaiser Permanente from 1995–1997. It is one of the largest investigations of childhood abuse, neglect, and household disfunction with later-life health and well-being negative outcomes. There were ten original ACEs divided into three main categories: Abuse, physical, emotion, and sexual' Neglect, physical and emotional; and Household Dysfunction, mental illness, domestic violence, divorce, incarcerated relative, and substance abuse. Numerous studies nationwide have been conducted on ACEs and trauma-informed care for children and youth and additional ACEs have been added to the list: witnessing violence, living in unsafe neighborhoods, experiencing racism, living in foster care, and experiencing bullying.

ACEs are traumatic events that occur in childhood. ACEs are linked to chronic health problems, mental illness, substance use problems, poor education outcomes, lack of job opportunities, and lower earning potential. Children and youth growing up with toxic stress (ACEs) may have difficulty forming healthy and stable relationships. For these reasons, there has been a national movement toward a more trauma-informed approach in areas such as public education, the criminal justice system, and the juvenile justice system. National, state, and local organizations have been formed to establish framework for trauma and introduce its concept of trauma and a trauma-informed approach to dealing with individuals, particularly, children and youth, in crisis, including evidence-based, trauma-informed services and education such as Crisis Intervention Team (CIT), TREM/MTREM, TARGET, ASCD Educational Leadership: Trauma Informed Teaching Strategies, Child Mind Institute: How Trauma Affects Kids in School, Teaching Tolerance: A Trauma-Informed Approach to Teaching Through Coronavirus, and the National Child Traumatic Stress Network: Child Trauma Toolkit for Educators.

The literature continues to grow about the effect of ACE and its clear link with criminal behaviors. What is yet to be determined is what role, if any, the juvenile justice system will play in accounting for and mitigating the effects of ACEs in sentencing while ensuring public safety and accountability.

REFERENCES

Felitti, V. J., Anda, R. F., Nordenbert, D., Willamson, D. F., Spitz, A. M., Edwards, V., Koss, M. P., & Marks, J. S. (1998). Relationship of childhood abuse and household dysfunction to many of the learning causes of death in adults: The adverse childhood experiences (ACE) study. *American Journal of Preventive Medicine, 14*(4), 245–258. https://www.ajpmonline.org/action/showPdf?pii=S0749-3797%2898%2900017-8

Harp, C. (2019). *Key amendments to the juvenile justice and delinquency prevention act made by the Juvenile Justice Reform Act of 2018.* U.S. Department of Justice. Office of Justice Programs. Office of Juvenile Justice and Delinquency Prevention.

Jensen, E. L., & Metsger, L. K. (1994). A test of the deterrent effect of legislative waiver on violent juvenile crime. *Crime and Delinquency, 40*, 96–104.

Lee, D. S., & McCrary, J. (2005). *Crime punishment, and myopia.* Paper 11491. Cambridge, MA: National Bureau of Economic Research.

Redding, R. E. (2010). *Juvenile transfer laws: An effective deterrent to delinquency?* U.S. Department of Justice. Office of Juvenile Programs. Office of Juvenile Justice and Delinquency Prevention.

Singer, S. I., & McDowall, D. (1988). Criminalizing delinquency: The deterrent effects of the New York juvenile offender law. *Law and Society Review, 22*, 521–535.

Index

About the Contributors

Riane M. Bolin is the graduate coordinator and an associate professor in the Department of Criminal Justice at Radford University. Her current research interests include a variety of issues related to juvenile justice and delinquency, including juvenile corrections, delinquency prevention, drug use, and victimization. Dr. Bolin's current projects involve the professional orientation of probation and parole officers as well as public opinion of blended sentencing.

Sheri Jenkins Keenan is the coordinator of the Center for Community Criminology & Research and clinical assistant professor in the Department of Criminology & Criminal Justice at the University of Memphis. She holds PhD, master of science, and bachelor of science in criminal justice, and a bachelor of arts in sociology. Dr. Keenan has fourteen years of experience in law enforcement and corrections. Her research interests focus on policing special populations with an emphasis on juveniles: delinquency, mental illness, school safety/prison pipeline, gangs/threat groups, ACEs, and juvenile justice program evaluation.

Addison Kobie is currently an MA student in the Department of Criminal Justice and Criminology at Sam Houston State University. She has a B.A. from Rockhurst University in criminal justice and psychology. Her research interests include, broadly, juvenile delinquency, program evaluations, and minority status within the criminal justice system.

Peter S. Lehmann is an assistant professor in the Department of Criminal Justice and Criminology at Sam Houston State University. His research interests include juvenile justice and delinquency, racial and ethnic disparities in sentencing, school discipline and safety, and public opinion on crime and criminal justice policy. His recently published work has appeared in *Justice Quarterly*, *Crime & Delinquency*, *Punishment & Society*, *Youth Violence and Juvenile Justice*, and other journals.

Lisa S. Nored is a professor of criminal justice at the University of Southern Mississippi (USM) where she serves as pre-law pathways coordinator in the College of Arts and Sciences. Dr. Nored earned undergraduate and graduate degrees in criminal justice from USM, JD from Mississippi College School of Law in 1996, and PhD in public policy and administration from Mississippi State University in 2007. Dr. Nored is an active researcher and has published extensively in the areas of justice policy and administration, child welfare, and juvenile justice. She is the author of twenty books, including legal treatises and textbooks, as well as more than thirty other publications. She has made more than fifty professional presentations. While at USM, Dr. Nored has generated over one million dollars in external funding. She was appointed to the Commission on Children's Justice by Chief Justice William L. Waller, Jr. and to the Mississippi State Advisory Group on Juvenile Justice by Governor Phil Bryant. Dr. Nored was also selected as a W. K. Kellogg Foundation Fellow and received specialized training in the field of child advocacy at the University of Michigan School of Law.

www.ingramcontent.com/pod-product-compliance
Ingram Content Group UK Ltd.
Pitfield, Milton Keynes, MK11 3LW, UK
UKHW020842290926
15470UKWH00004B/1502

9 781793 62363